T0386690

BETWEEN
THE
SHEETS

To my parents, George and Margo, my siblings, James and Nicola, my treasured wider family, dear friends and cherished loved ones lost before this book hit the shelves, all of whom I kept this a secret from. Surprise! I hope you can all forgive me.

BETWEEN THE SHEETS

EASY AND INVENTIVE LAYERED TRAYBAKES

SARAH WORDIE

murdoch books
London | Sydney

INTRODUCTION 6

MEAT 12

FISH & SEAFOOD 42

VEGETARIAN & VEGAN 62

SWEET 88

CELEBRATIONS 110

INDEX 138

ACKNOWLEDGEMENTS 143

RECIPE NOTES 144

INTRODUCTION

I was born and brought up on a farm in the north-east of Scotland where my family's lives revolved around food, from the animals Dad raised to the home-cooked meals Mum would rustle up. My family recall my healthy appetite as a youngster, with my eyes being 'bigger than my stomach'. Cooking, and baking in particular, became an activity I spent many an hour on. It grew into a competitive sport; I'd enter local contests with my scones or cakes, taking on county-show veterans.

When the time came to move to study medicine at university, I was faced with a new cooking challenge. I needed to make meals that were quick, easy and – most importantly – achievable within a student budget. I loved hosting dinner parties with flatmates, cooking simple dishes that were tasty yet inexpensive.

In December 2016, we planned an all-out Christmas dinner for fifteen friends. On the day of the party, we realised no one had bought the turkey. We were missing the centrepiece of our Christmas meal. I was pacing the virtually empty supermarket aisles, trying to prevent an impending dining disaster, when my eyes were drawn to turkey mince. As I stared at the packets that could potentially salvage the dinner, I constructed a meal in my head. A one-pan layered dish that included 'pigs in blankets', Brussels sprouts and cranberry sauce alongside the turkey mince. The dinner party was rescued from the brink of disaster and the Christmas Dinner Lasagne (page 112) was the talking point of the party. The novelty of this idea took hold and I went on to create other innovative lasagnes, including the Chicken Tikka 'Masalasagne' (page 24) and my infamous Fish and Chips Lasagne (page 46).

Throughout university, I joked that one day I'd write a cookbook all about lasagnes, layered dishes that were tasty, time-saving and budget friendly. Then along came a certain cookery TV show, hosted by Jamie Oliver. I entered on a whim, thinking that my idea of creating novelty lasagnes wouldn't come to anything. However, I made the final six and cooked some of my unconventional lasagnes on national TV. I cooked for industry leading experts and served my Christmas Dinner Lasagne to Jamie himself.

After this whirlwind, I focused on making my student dream of writing a cookbook a reality. *Between the Sheets* is a practical yet fun cookbook full of recipes for simple, layered dishes that even inexperienced cooks can make. I honestly believe this book has something for all. There are simple lasagnes to make for a midweek supper when time really is of the essence, ranging to slightly more complex recipes that you can spend time assembling for a dinner party to impress friends. There is even a celebrations chapter that has a lasagne idea for occasions throughout the year, whether that be St Patrick's Day right through to Bonfire Night. This book offers a lasagne for everyone and every day. The novelty of making tasty, eye-catching, speedy recipes in a layered way is appealing to many. What's more, I think cooking should be fun. We shouldn't be slaving away trying to create perfect puff pastry or crispy crêpes. Instead I suggest shortcuts throughout that enable you to whip up delicious traybakes that won't break your bank balance or back.

TIPS AND TRICKS

One understandable apprehension is that making a lasagne is a time-consuming, laborious activity. The prospect of a dozen pots and pans to wash up is daunting, so a lasagne is often considered a luxury meal for when eating out. I want to show how it doesn't have to be like that. There are simple tricks and nifty techniques that allow you to create a layered meal in no time at all. This book pushes the boundaries of what is a lasagne, with the running theme being the concept of layering. Iconic dishes from various cuisines can be enjoyed in a one-dish, layered-up way, thereby reimagining how you might conventionally enjoy the likes of a Sunday roast, a quesadilla or even an espresso martini.

Almost all the following recipes use a 25 x 20-cm (10 x 8-inch) ovenproof dish, which gives you between four and six servings, allowing you to throw together a tasty, layered dish for family, friends or flatmates. The majority of the recipes are best enjoyed fresh on the day of assembly as the 'sheets' absorb liquid from the fillings, potentially leaving you with a structurally unsound, soggy dish. Conversely, there are some saucy recipes that may well thicken up if portions are left for a second day. To avoid either soggy bottoms or shrivelled-up sheets, I recommend enjoying each lasagne on the day of its creation.

THE LAYERS

I've talked a lot about the layering concept that is the basis for this book, so I want to give you some examples of 'sheets' that I've used in the recipes. Some are expected, while others you might find surprising, but I promise all work in making these dishes look and taste fantastic.

First up, pastry. In all its forms, pastry makes an exceptional layer. Whether it be crispy filo (phyllo) pastry, which is wonderful in both sweet and savoury dishes, buttery puff pastry in a delightful millefeuille-like lasagne, through to shortcrust acting as a shell that encases a rich and fruity traybake. Pancakes, both the American style and French crêpe versions, make a perfect sheet. These dishes can be enjoyed hot or cold and with a multitude of fillings from custard to curd. Sticking with sweet sheets, a biscuit can bring structure to these dishes. The classic digestive biscuit (graham cracker) is an exemplary example of such a sheet, providing a degree of support to the traybakes and yet also absorbing the flavours from the filling so perfectly. Other crumbly and crispy crackers that are used throughout the book include the quintessentially British custard cream, the archetypal Scottish shortbread and, lastly, a gorgeously gooey chocolate chip cookie.

Next in this whistle-stop tour of layers are some doughy delights. Ranging from muffins to hot cross buns and crusty loaves of bread

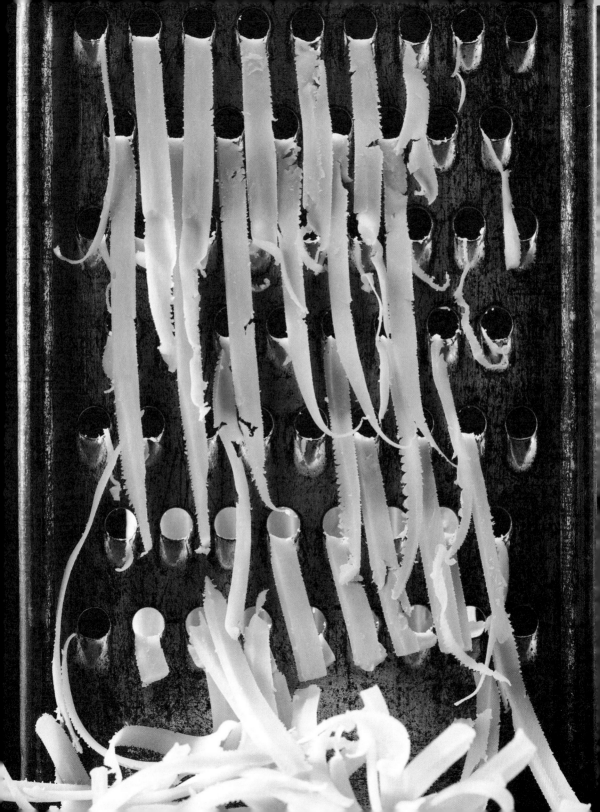

to donuts, all these baked goods make an excellent sheet as they are ideal at maximising the moistness of these lasagnes.

You might be a sweet treat lover, like me, but savoury layers can be just as inventive. The humble potato is a staple, although it's often considered rather dull 'plate filler'. The trusty spud provides architectural stability as a layer while being versatile with flavours and fillings. From courgettes (zucchini) to aubergines (eggplants), using vegetables as the layer speaks to the doctor in me. I'm proud to create recipes that are packed with goodness, so you achieve your five-a-day without even realising. Moving on to a wider category of layers, we need to talk about those flour-based ones. Who would have thought simple pitas, naans and tortillas could really spice up recipes while providing the vital structure that is essential in some of these dishes. And now for some rather unique 'sheets', including the classic Yorkshire pudding, the archetypal Indian poppadom and the Scottish breakfast favourite, the potato scone, all of which I promise make the dishes pleasing to both the eye and stomach. Now last, but no means least, the epitomical layer of the classic lasagne is pasta, which of course features frequently in its traditional form in many recipes, but other varieties do appear with one recipe using ravioli, while in another macaroni cheese makes a tasty appearance.

THE FILLINGS

We all know and love the traditional lasagne with a rich ragù and creamy sauce, but I show there are endless possibilities for what can be used to fill between the sheets. I want to introduce some quick hacks that will really speed up the process of assembling a lasagne.

Firstly, the classic béchamel involves melting, stirring and whisking, whereas I often use a ricotta-based sauce instead. Mix soft cheese with some milk and then add the flavours you like, whether that be herbs, spices or additional cheeses. You can make a similar sauce using crème fraîche, which acts as a neutral base that you can add flavours to depending on whether it's a savoury or sweet lasagne you're making. What is also great about this basic recipe is it can be made fully vegan, using a plant-based soft cheese or crème fraîche and milk. Just make sure they are the unsweetened variety.

Additionally, a go-to tomato sauce can elevate a good recipe to a great one. Canned tomatoes are one ingredient I try not to scrimp on. For most ingredients used in these recipes, the basic or budget ranges available in supermarkets work perfectly well, but canned tomatoes are one of only a handful of items I might splurge on as I find them less bitter tasting than some of the cheaper alternatives. The addition of herbs, from thyme to rosemary or basil to bay leaves, elevates the flavours in the sauce and I regularly interchange fresh or dried, depending on what I have to hand. Just note that dried herbs have a more concentrated flavour so you need a smaller quantity than when using the fresh option. A lazy cheat I sometimes use in a basic tomato sauce is store-bought garlic paste instead of fresh cloves; it gives a punchier taste and saves the hassle of dicing the fiddly cloves.

Another time-saving trick in many recipes is to use either canned or frozen vegetables, fruit or fish as these can be cheaper and tend to be pre-prepared, so you can just chuck them into the pan. Similarly, a hack I swear by is using pots of spice paste or jars of sauces, from Massaman curry paste through to sweet and sour sauce. It reduces the time you spend labouring away while minimising the more niche ingredients you would end up buying to use just the once.

FINAL THOUGHTS

My aim is that this book caters for everyone. A number of recipes can easily be made meat-free by substituting extra vegetables, tofu or other plant-based alternatives. The recipes can also be adapted to suit specific dietary needs, such as gluten- or dairy-free, by exchanging the listed ingredients for the free-from ranges available in the majority of supermarkets. Ingredients like wheat-free lasagne sheets or oat fraîche provide excellent substitutes.

Throughout the book, I make suggestions to reduce food waste by using up leftovers as part of the fillings in lasagnes and traybakes. For example, by using the spare meat or vegetables left over from a roast dinner (pages 16 and 30), including your Christmas Day dinner trimmings (page 112), through to day-old muffins found lurking in the cake tin (page 96). As well as minimising food waste, these recipes give any leftovers an innovative, tasty, new lease of life.

Additionally, many of the ingredients, especially the spices or sauces, are used over and over again throughout this book, so you don't have to buy a product to only use it once. I am also very proud of the fact that the overwhelming majority of ingredients were bought from a standard supermarket, therefore not requiring specialist shops or multiple trips.

Also key is the seasonality of produce in these fillings. Whether it is rhubarb in the spring or strawberries in the summer, make these dishes when the ingredients are at their very best.

Finally, I wrote this book to be a fun, unique approach to serving dishes ranging from everyday comfort food to more refined, elegant dinner-party or date-night meals in a novel, layered, one-pan way. I hope you enjoy devouring these recipes and that *Between the Sheets* becomes your new go-to cookbook.

MEAT

CHICKEN, PRUNE AND PISTACHIO LASAGNE

In rural Scotland, we often ate pheasant as it was very accessible. Originally, I used lean pheasant in this lasagne – an incredible combination with prunes and pistachios – but now I live in a city, access to pheasant is limited. So, I've swapped it for chicken as it complements those sweet, nutty flavours.

Serves 4

3 tablespoons vegetable oil

8 pancetta rashers, sliced

1 small leek, finely chopped

3 thyme sprigs

500g (1lb 2oz) skinless, boneless chicken thighs

20g (¾oz) plain (all-purpose) flour

500g (1lb 2oz) mushrooms, sliced

150ml (5½fl oz) red wine

300ml (10½fl oz) chicken stock

150ml (5½fl oz) double (heavy) cream

2 tablespoons wholegrain mustard

100g (3½oz) prunes, pitted and halved

15g (½oz) cornflour (cornstarch), mixed with 1 teaspoon cold water (optional)

8–10 dried lasagne sheets

Handful of shelled, unsalted pistachios, finely chopped

Salt and freshly ground black pepper

Preheat the oven to 200°C/180°C fan/390°F/gas 6.

Heat 2 tablespoons oil in a frying pan (skillet) over a medium heat. Add the pancetta and fry until it starts to colour. Add the leek and thyme, then cook for 5 minutes or until the leeks are soft and the pancetta is crisp. Leaving any oil in the pan, transfer the pancetta and leeks to a bowl and set aside.

Cut the chicken into small pieces, place in a separate bowl and coat in the flour. Warm the remaining 1 tablespoon oil in the frying pan. Add the chicken and cook for 3 minutes or until browned on all sides. Add the mushrooms and sauté for 5 minutes or until soft.

Pour in the wine, stock and cream, then add the mustard and prunes. Simmer on a low heat for 20 minutes or until the sauce has thickened. If it's too runny, add a little cornflour. Fold the leeks and pancetta into the sauce. Season with salt and pepper to taste.

Spoon a little sauce from the pan into a 25 x 20-cm (10 x 8-inch) ovenproof dish. Cover the base of the dish with a layer of lasagne sheets. Trim the sheets to fit the dish, if necessary. Top with half of the chicken and prune mixture. Repeat these layers once more, reserving 3 tablespoons of the sauce. Finish with a third layer of lasagne sheets, then cover the pasta with the reserved sauce.

Bake in the hot oven for 45 minutes or until the pasta is cooked through and the lasagne is bubbling. If the top is browning before the lasagne is fully cooked, cover with foil. In the final 10 minutes of cooking, scatter the pistachios over the top and return to the oven. Allow to cool for 5 minutes before slicing and serving.

SWEET AND SOUR PORK LASAGNE

A regular meal in many households, I've taken the key components of this family favourite and turned it into a one-dish lasagne. With a few shortcuts, my sweet and sour pork is as easy as is possible. This may be a controversial question: Are you 'team pro-pineapple' or 'team no-pineapple'? The addition of this divisive ingredient is at your discretion, although I very much think it should be included...

Serves 4

2 tablespoons vegetable oil

1 red onion, chopped into wedges

3-cm (1-inch) piece fresh root ginger, peeled and diced

1 large red (bell) pepper, chopped into bite-size chunks

425g (15oz) pork leg, diced

1 x 500-g (18-oz) jar sweet and sour sauce

1 x 100-g (3½-oz) can pineapple chunks in natural juice

2 carrots, peeled and grated (shredded)

2 x 250-g (9-oz) pouches microwaveable brown basmati rice

30g (1oz) cashew nuts, roughly chopped

1 x 60-g (2-oz) bag prawn crackers, to serve

Preheat the oven to 200°C/180°C fan/390°F/gas 6.

Heat the oil in a large frying pan (skillet). Add the onion, ginger and red pepper and fry for 5 minutes or until tender. Next, add the diced pork to the pan and, stirring occasionally, fry for 2 minutes or until browned on all sides.

Pour the sweet and sour sauce into the pan and stir well. If using, drain the pineapple chunks and set aside, reserving the juice. Add 75ml (2½fl oz) of the pineapple juice to the pan, stir and simmer on a low heat for 15 minutes. (If you're not adding pineapple, add 75ml (2½fl oz) water instead.) Lastly, add the grated carrots and pineapple chunks to the pan and simmer while stirring for a further 2 minutes.

Cover the base of a 25 x 20-cm (10 x 8-inch) ovenproof dish with one-third of the rice. Top with half of the sweet and sour pork.

Repeat the layers of rice and pork once more. Finish with a third layer of rice.

Cover the dish with foil and bake the lasagne in the hot oven for 45 minutes. Remove the foil from the dish, scatter the cashew nuts over the top and return to the oven for a further 10 minutes.

Remove the dish from the oven and allow the lasagne to cool for a few minutes before serving with prawn crackers on the side.

COOK'S TIP If you have any meat left over from a roast dinner, feel free to use that instead. Chicken is a delicious alternative to pork, and tofu is an excellent meat-free option.

PULLED PORK NACHO BAKE

Smoky and sticky, this barbecue pulled pork bake is marvellous but messy! This sharing dish is perfect for a relaxed supper with friends or even eaten cold at a picnic – everyone can dig into this one-dish delight. I like to serve this bake with a peppery rocket (arugula) and sweet orange salad, drizzled with a tangy citrus dressing, which complements the smoky barbecue flavours.

Serves 4

Slow-cooked barbecue pulled pork shoulder (approx. 900g/2lb, available from all major supermarkets)

2 small red onions, chopped

2 red (bell) peppers, chopped

3 tablespoons vegetable oil

8 tablespoons barbecue sauce

1 x 200-g (7-oz) bag tortilla chips or nachos

1 mozzarella ball, roughly torn

Preheat the oven to 200°C/180°C fan/390°F/gas 6.

Cook the barbecue pulled pork following the instructions on the packaging. Once cooked, shred the meat by pulling it apart with two forks.

Place the chopped onions and red peppers in a roasting tray (sheet pan) and drizzle over the oil. Roast the vegetables in the hot oven for 20 minutes. Remove the tray from the oven, drizzle 4 tablespoons of the barbecue sauce over the roasted vegetables and return to the oven for a further 5 minutes.

Cover the base of a 25 x 20-cm (10 x 8-inch) ovenproof dish with a layer of tortilla chips or nachos. Top the chips with half of the pulled pork and then half of the roasted vegetables. Repeat these layers once more. Finish with a third layer of tortilla chips. Drizzle another 4 tablespoons of barbecue sauce over the top of the bake, then tear over the mozzarella, dotting small chunks across the surface.

Place the ovenproof dish on a baking tray and bake in the hot oven for 20 minutes or until the mozzarella has melted.

Remove the dish from the oven and either eat straight away while warm or allow to cool and enjoy cold.

COOK'S TIP You can always make your own slow-cooked pulled pork from scratch. Buy a pork shoulder joint that is approximately 1kg (2lb 3oz) and follow your favourite recipes – you can find any number of recipes online.

FULL ENGLISH BREAKFAST LASAGNE

The ultimate comfort food, this one-dish take on the Full English Breakfast is naughty but so very nice. It's packed with all your favourite breakfast bites, making it the ideal weekend brunch. What's more, it takes minutes to assemble and you can leave it to cook away while you enjoy a freshly brewed pot of tea. Serve with your favourite sauce, whether that be the red or the brown one.

Serves 4

4 pork sausages

8 potato scones

1 tablespoon vegetable oil

300g (10½oz) mushrooms, roughly sliced

100g (3½oz) black pudding, roughly chopped

2 x 400-g (14-oz) cans baked beans

4 back bacon rashers

8 hash browns

3 large eggs

75ml (2½fl oz) double (heavy) cream

50ml (1¾fl oz) milk

4 thyme sprigs

12 cherry tomatoes

Preheat the oven to 200°C/180°C fan/390°F/gas 6.

Place the sausages in a roasting tray (sheet pan) and bake in the hot oven for 10 minutes to partially cook. Remove the tray from the oven and, once cool, cut the sausages in half lengthways.

Using a rolling pin, slightly flatten out the potato scones.

Heat the oil in a frying pan (skillet) over a high heat. Add the sliced mushrooms and, stirring occasionally, cook for a few minutes until golden. Remove the pan from the heat and set aside.

Cover the base of a 30 x 23-cm (12 x 9-inch) ovenproof dish with 4 potato scones. If necessary, trim the scones to fit the dish. Next, add the sausages in a layer, then crumble over the black pudding pieces. Pour over the first can of baked beans. Cover the beans with another 4 potato scones. Next, add the mushrooms in a layer, then arrange the bacon on top. Pour over the second can of baked beans. Lastly, top with the hash browns.

Whisk the eggs, cream and milk in a bowl. Strip the leaves from three-quarters of the thyme sprigs and stir into the mixture, setting aside the rest for later, and season well with pepper. Pour this eggy mixture over the assembled lasagne to fill the dish.

Place the ovenproof dish on a baking tray and bake in the hot oven for 30 minutes or until the egg is cooked. Scatter the cherry tomatoes over the top and bake for a further 10 minutes or until the lasagne is bubbling and the tomatoes are soft and juicy. Remove the dish from the oven, scatter over the reserved thyme leaves and allow to cool for 2 minutes before slicing and serving.

CRISPY DUCK PANCAKE LASAGNE

A twist on the takeaway classic. Conventional crispy duck pancakes are so tasty, but often messy to eat, which is why I've taken the traditional flavours and turned them into this one-dish lasagne with the addition of a crispy slaw layered between the pancake sheets. With only a handful of ingredients and a few simple steps to follow, this sharing dish is a perfect substitute for a Friday-night takeaway.

Serves 6

2 crispy aromatic half ducks (available from major supermarkets)

1 jar (approx. 300g/10½oz) hoisin sauce

150g (5½oz) pickled red cabbage, drained

2 carrots, peeled and grated (shredded)

6 spring onions (scallions), finely sliced, plus extra curls to serve

12–15 Chinese-style pancakes

10g (⅓oz) toasted sesame seeds

Preheat the oven to 200°C/180°C fan/390°F/gas 6.

Cook the duck halves following the instructions on the packaging. Once cooked, remove the skin and shred the meat by pulling it apart with two forks. Place the shredded duck in a bowl, add 100g (3½oz) hoisin sauce and stir to coat all the meat.

To make the slaw, place the pickled red cabbage, grated carrots and sliced spring onions in a large bowl. Add 100g (3½oz) hoisin sauce and stir until fully combined.

Cover the base of a 25 x 20-cm (10 x 8-inch) ovenproof dish with 4 or 5 pancakes; as the pancakes are thin and delicate, overlap each pancake to make the layer more robust. Top with half of the shredded duck and then half of the slaw. Repeat these layers of once more. Finish with a third layer of pancakes. Pour over the remaining 100g (3½oz) hoisin sauce, spread to cover the top layer of pancakes and then cover the dish with foil.

Bake in the hot oven for 20–25 minutes or until the lasagne is bubbling. Remove the foil, scatter the sesame seeds over the top and return to the oven for a further 5 minutes.

Remove the dish from the oven and allow the lasagne to cool for a few minutes before scattering over a handful of spring onion curls, then slicing and serving.

COOK'S TIP You can buy aromatic crispy duck in supermarkets, and often it includes pancakes and hoisin sauce. Alternatively, you can slow-cook duck legs in aromatic spices to create your own crispy duck from scratch, and buy pancakes and sauce separately.

CHORIZO, TOMATO, OLIVE AND GNOCCHI TRAYBAKE

This easy traybake uses a number of storecupboard staples and, more importantly, can be made in minutes, saving you both time and effort. Adapt it for vegetarians by simply exchanging the chorizo for some of your favourite herby, plant-based sausages or by adding extra vegetables instead. While I've used goats' cheese, this dish also works really well with a crumbly feta or creamy mozzarella.

Serves 4

2 tablespoons olive oil

1 onion, finely chopped

200g (7oz) chorizo, chopped

125g (4½oz) pitted olives, halved

125g (4½oz) sundried tomatoes, drained and chopped

1 x 400-g (14-oz) can baked beans

150ml (5½fl oz) red wine

500ml (17fl oz) tomato passata (strained tomatoes)

20 cherry tomatoes, halved

1kg (2lb 3oz) gnocchi

75g (2½oz) goats' cheese

Handful of fresh basil, roughly chopped

Preheat the oven to 200°C/180°C fan/390°F/gas 6.

Heat the oil in a large saucepan over a medium heat. Add the onion and cook for 5 minutes or until softened. Add the chorizo and cook for a further 3 minutes or until crisp. Next, tip in the olives and sundried tomatoes and cook for a further 1 minute.

Reduce the heat to low and stir in the baked beans. Pour the red wine and tomato passata into the pan. Simmer on a low heat for 15–20 minutes or until the sauce has reduced and thickened. Lastly, add the cherry tomatoes and cook for a further 5 minutes.

Cover the base of a 25 x 20-cm (10 x 8-inch) ovenproof dish with one-third of the gnocchi. Top the gnocchi with half of the chorizo mixture. Crumble 25g (¾oz) goats' cheese on top. Repeat the layers once more. Finish with a third layer of gnocchi, then crumble over the remaining goats' cheese.

Bake in the hot oven for 20–30 minutes or until the gnocchi are soft, the cheese has melted and the lasagne is bubbling.

Remove the dish from the oven and allow the traybake to cool for a few minutes. Serve with chopped basil sprinkled on top.

COOK'S TIP There is no need to pre-cook the gnocchi. Simply place it in the ovenproof dish directly from the packet. To test the gnocchi is cooked, pierce one piece with the tip of a sharp knife – it should be soft in texture.

VENISON, MUSHROOM AND FIG LASAGNE

Venison is an overlooked ingredient; however, I hope this lasagne becomes a firm favourite even though it can be more expensive than other meats, With layers of lean venison, fruity figs and earthy mushrooms nestled in a rich red wine sauce, this lasagne is the ultimate midwinter meal. Diced steak or mince work in this recipe. If you do use mince, make sure you add some flour to thicken the sauce.

Serves 4

2 tablespoons vegetable oil

1 onion, finely chopped

3 rosemary sprigs

10 whole juniper berries

2 bay leaves

200g (7oz) bacon lardons

500g (1lb 2oz) venison steak, diced

30g (1oz) plain (all-purpose) flour

200g (7oz) chestnut button mushrooms, halved

300ml (10½fl oz) red wine

450ml (15fl oz) beef stock

2 heaped tablespoons redcurrant jelly

6 figs, cut into quarters

800g (1lb 12oz) potatoes, peeled and cut into 2-mm (¹⁄₁₆-inch) thick slices

Salt and freshly ground black pepper

200g (7oz) Tenderstem broccoli, griddled, to serve

Heat the oil in a frying pan (skillet) over a medium heat. Add the onion and cook for 2 minutes. Add the rosemary, juniper berries, bay leaves and bacon lardons, then brown for 5 minutes.

Place the venison in a separate bowl, sprinkle over the flour and stir to coat. Add the venison to the pan and cook for 2 minutes or until browned on all sides. Add the mushrooms and, stirring occasionally, fry for a further 5 minutes or until softened.

Reduce the heat to low and pour in the wine, stock and redcurrant jelly. Simmer for 30 minutes or until the sauce has reduced. In the final 5 minutes, add the figs, reserving a handful of pieces. Remove the pan from the heat and discard the rosemary, juniper and bay leaves. Season with salt and pepper to taste.

Preheat the oven to 220°C/200°C fan/430°F/gas 7.

Cover the base of a 25 x 20-cm (10 x 8-inch) ovenproof dish with a layer of potato slices. Top the potatoes with half of the venison and red wine sauce. Repeat these layers once more, reserving 3 tablespoons of the red wine sauce. Finish with a third layer of potato slices and pour over the reserved red wine sauce.

Bake in the hot oven for 1 hour or until the potatoes are cooked through and the lasagne is bubbling. If the top browns before the potatoes softened, cover with foil. In the final 10 minutes, scatter the reserved figs over the top and return to the oven.

Remove the dish from the oven and allow to cool for 5 minutes before slicing and serving with griddled Tenderstem broccoli.

CHICKEN TIKKA 'MASALASAGNE'

This was one of the first ever lasagne-style recipes that I made in one tray, and so I had to include it in this book. When I was a student, I would cook this for my flatmates. Using naan bread and poppadoms instead of a pasta layer adds the fun factor to a lasagne, and it's a really simple way to serve up a one-pot curry. If you like, add a few chopped fresh red chillies when cooking the onions.

Serves 4

2 tablespoons vegetable oil

1 onion, roughly chopped

2 red (bell) peppers, roughly chopped

500g (1lb 2oz) chicken thighs, chopped into bite-size chunks

1 x 200-g (7-oz) jar tikka masala paste

1 x 200-g (7-oz) can chopped tomatoes

125ml (4½fl oz) double (heavy) cream

150g (5½oz) natural yogurt

4 roti (or you can use naan or chapati)

6 tablespoons mango chutney

2 poppadoms, plus extra to serve

Place the oil in a large frying pan (skillet) over a medium heat. Add the onion and cook for 2 minutes then add the red peppers. Stir to combine and cook for a further 5 minutes until the peppers are slightly softened. Add the diced chicken and cook for 3 minutes until browned all over.

Reduce the heat to low and add the tikka masala paste, chopped tomatoes, cream and yogurt. Stir well to make sure all the ingredients are fully combined and leave to simmer for 20 minutes, stirring occasionally. The sauce should thicken in consistency. Remove the pan from the heat and set aside.

Preheat the oven to 200°C/180°C fan/390°F/gas 6.

Cover the base of a 30-cm (12-inch) ovenproof frying pan (skillet) with a layer of roti. Alternatively, use a 25 x 20-cm (10 x 8-inch) ovenproof dish. Top the roti with half of the chicken tikka curry mixture and then 2 tablespoons of the mango chutney.

Repeat the layers of roti, chicken tikka curry and mango chutney once more. Finish with a final layer of poppadoms, breaking them up to fit the dish.

Bake the lasagne in the oven for 30 minutes.

Remove the dish from the oven and allow the lasagne to cool for 5 minutes before serving with the remaining mango chutney.

SPICED LAMB LASAGNE

Taking inspiration from the cuisines of North Africa, this lasagne pairs aromatic lamb with sweet apricots. Zesty ricotta and crisp aubergines (eggplants) provide extra layers in this delicious dish. Enjoy this first as a midweek supper, then any leftovers provide a perfect lunch for the following day.

Serves 4

400g (14oz) lamb shoulder, diced

1½ teaspoons ground cumin

½ teaspoon ground turmeric

½ teaspoon ground ginger

½ teaspoon smoked paprika

6 tablespoons vegetable oil, plus extra for brushing

2 large aubergines (eggplants), sliced into thin discs

1 onion, finely diced

100g (3½oz) dried apricots, halved

150g (5½oz) orzo

3 tablespoons apricot jam (preserve)

1 tablespoon tomato paste (concentrated purée)

500ml (17fl oz) chicken stock

100ml (3½fl oz) red wine

250g (9oz) ricotta cheese

125ml (4½fl oz) double (heavy) cream

Zest and juice of 1 lime

25g (¾oz) Parmesan cheese, grated (shredded)

Mint leaves, to serve

Place the diced lamb in a mixing bowl and add the ground spices. Toss to coat the meat evenly in the spices and leave to marinate for at least 30 minutes or longer, if you have the time.

Heat a frying pan (skillet) over a high heat. Drizzle 4 tablespoons of oil over both sides of the aubergine (eggplant) slices and fry in small batches for 5 minutes on each side or until golden brown.

Heat 2 tablespoons oil in the same pan over a medium heat. Add the onion and cook for 2 minutes, then add the lamb and cook, stirring, to brown on all sides. Reduce the heat to low and add the apricots and orzo, then stir in the apricot jam and tomato paste.

Add the stock and wine. Season well and leave to simmer over a low heat for 20 minutes, stirring occasionally to stop the orzo sticking to the pan. Add a splash of water if the sauce is too thick.

In a separate bowl, combine the ricotta and cream. Stir in the zest and juice from the lime.

Preheat the oven to 200°C/180°C fan/390°F/gas 6.

Brush the sides and base of a 25 x 20-cm (10 x 8-inch) ovenproof dish and cover with a layer of the aubergine slices. Spoon over half of the lamb and orzo mixture and then top with half of the ricotta sauce. Repeat these layers once more. Finish with a third layer of aubergine slices. Scatter the Parmesan cheese over the top layer of aubergine.

Bake in the hot oven for 40–45 minutes or until the aubergine is cooked through and the cheese is golden. Remove the dish from the oven and allow the lasagne to cool for 5 minutes before scattering over a few mint leaves, then slicing and serving.

SPICY MEATBALL LASAGNE

Out of all the recipes in this book, this one is the closest to the classic lasagne we all know and love. I've made a few subtle changes and incorporated sneaky shortcuts to reduce the time you'd usually spend making the traditional ragù and béchamel sauces. Gone are the days of tirelessly stirring a sauce or having half a dozen pans to wash up. This simple lasagne will be devoured by all.

Serves 4

3 tablespoons olive oil

16 beef meatballs (available in all supermarkets)

1 onion, finely chopped

3 garlic cloves, diced

3 red chillies, deseeded and chopped

2 teaspoons dried oregano

100ml (3½fl oz) red wine

500g (1lb 2oz) tomato passata (strained tomatoes)

2 teaspoon caster (superfine) sugar

250g (9oz) ricotta cheese

75g (2½oz) Parmesan cheese, grated (shredded)

100ml (3½fl oz) milk

6 fresh lasagne sheets, cut to size

1 mozzarella ball, torn into chunks

Salt and freshly ground black pepper

Garlic bread, to serve

Preheat the oven to 200°C/180°C fan/390°F/gas 6.

Heat the oil in a frying pan (skillet) over a medium heat. Flatten the meatballs slightly with the back of a spoon (this prevents them running off when assembling the lasagne). Add the meatballs to the pan and brown them all over. Leaving any oil in the pan, transfer the meatballs to a plate and set aside.

Reduce the heat slightly. Add the onion, garlic and chillies to the pan and cook for 3 minutes or until softened. Add the oregano and wine, then simmer for 2 minutes. Add the passata and sugar, then simmer for 15–20 minutes or until thickened. Season well. Remove from the heat and return the meatballs to the pan.

Mix together the ricotta, 50g (1¾oz) Parmesan and the milk in a small bowl until fully combined.

Cover the base of a 25 x 20-cm (10 x 8-inch) ovenproof dish with a layer of lasagne sheets. Trim the sheets to fit the dish, if necessary. Top the pasta with 8 meatballs in tomato sauce, arranging them evenly across the dish. Dot the surface with one-third of the mozzarella and pour over one-third of the ricotta sauce. Repeat the layers once more. Finish with a third layer of lasagne, then cover with the remaining ricotta sauce. Scatter over the remaining mozzarella and grated Parmesan cheese.

Place the ovenproof dish on a baking tray and bake in the hot oven for 30–40 minutes or until the lasagne is bubbling. Remove the dish from the oven and allow the lasagne to cool for 5 minutes before slicing and serving with plenty of garlic bread.

SAUSAGE, AUBERGINE AND PUY LENTIL LASAGNE

Super-simple and speedy, this lasagne solves your midweek dinner dilemmas. You can even prepare the main components ahead of time, and by using pouches of lentils, this dish can be assembled in 5 minutes. The leftovers, if you're lucky to have some, make an excellent next-day lunch. And if you're cutting down on meat, swap out the sausages for tempeh or even cauliflower.

Serves 4

2 tablespoons sunflower oil

8 pork sausages

1 large onion, chopped

3 garlic cloves

2 aubergines (eggplants), cut into bite-size chunks

2 x 400-g (14-oz) cans chopped tomatoes

2 teaspoons dried mixed herbs

2 teaspoons caster (superfine) sugar

2 x 250-g (9-oz) pouches ready-cooked Puy lentils

150g (5½oz) goats' cheese

Salt and freshly ground black pepper

Crusty sourdough loaf, to serve

Preheat the oven to 200°C/180°C fan/390°F/gas 6.

Heat the oil in a large frying pan (skillet) over a medium heat. Add the sausages to the pan and cook for a couple of minutes, tossing them around in the pan to brown them all over. Remove the sausages from the pan and allow to cool before chopping each one into 4 or 5 pieces.

Add the onion and garlic to the same pan and cook for a couple of minutes. Stir in the aubergine and cook for a further 3 minutes or until slightly softened. Pour in the chopped tomatoes, then sprinkle in the herbs and sugar. Rinse out each tomato can with around 50ml (1¾fl oz) cold water and add this to the pan, too. Simmer on a low heat for 15 minutes, allowing the sauce to thicken. Add the chopped sausages and cook for a further 5 minutes. Season with salt and pepper to taste.

Cover the base of a 25 x 20-cm (10 x 8-inch) ovenproof dish with one-third of the lentils. Top the lentils with half of the sausage and aubergine mixture. Next, cover the layer with 50g (1¾oz) goats' cheese. Repeat the layers once more. Finish with a third layer of lentils. Dot the surface with the remaining goats' cheese.

Cover the dish with foil and bake in the hot oven for 30 minutes or until the cheese has melted and the lasagne is bubbling.

Remove the dish from the oven and allow the lasagne to cool for 5 minutes before slicing and serving with slices of sourdough bread to mop up the sauce.

ROAST DINNER LASAGNE

Recently Yorkshire pudding wraps were a foodie phenomenon, and I use them as layers in this dish just as you would use pasta sheets in a traditional lasagne. If you make your Yorkshire puddings from scratch, just roll them out flat. I make this dish with roast beef and horseradish sauce, but you can easily use lamb with mint jelly or chicken with bread sauce instead. These vegetables are my roast-beef-dinner favourites, but feel free to change it up and throw in whatever you have lurking in your kitchen. This all-in-one, roast dinner lasagne is perfect for using up any leftovers, so if that's the route you're taking, jump straight to the instructions for assembling and baking the lasagne.

Serves 6–8

For the cauliflower cheese

300g (10½oz) cauliflower florets (approx. half a head), chopped into bite-size pieces

30g (1oz) butter

30g (1oz) plain (all-purpose) flour

300ml (10½fl oz) milk

100g (3½oz) Cheddar cheese, grated (shredded)

Salt and freshly ground black pepper

For the beef

500g (1lb 2oz) beef topside

2 teaspoons Dijon mustard

Preheat the oven to 240°C/220°C fan/465°F/gas 9.

To make the cauliflower cheese, bring a saucepan of salted water to the boil. Add the cauliflower florets and cook for 5 minutes or until parboiled. Drain the cauliflower and set aside for later.

Put the same pan back over a low heat. Melt the butter, then stir in the flour until thick and buttery. Whisking continuously, slowly add the milk to make a sauce. Bubble the sauce for 2 minutes to thicken and then stir in 75g (2½oz) Cheddar. Season to taste.

Remove the pan from the heat, add the cooked cauliflower florets and stir to coat them in the sauce. Check the seasoning and then tip the cauliflower cheese mixture into an ovenproof dish and top with the remaining cheese.

Place the dish in the hot oven for 15 minutes or until the cheese has melted and the sauce is bubbling. Set aside for later.

Meanwhile, place the beef joint in a roasting tray (sheet pan) and spread the mustard over the top. Place the tray in the hot oven and roast the beef at 240°C/220°C fan/465°F/gas 9 for 10 minutes. Reduce the heat to 180°C/160°C fan/350°F/gas 4 and cook for a further 20–25 minutes.

Remove the tray from the oven, cover the beef with foil and allow the beef to rest for at least 30 minutes. Once rested, carve the beef into thin 2–3-mm (1/16–1/8-inch) slices.

Continued overleaf

For the roast potatoes

2 tablespoons vegetable oil

275g (10oz) Maris Piper potatoes, peeled and cut into 3-cm (1-inch) cubes

1 teaspoon coarse sea salt flakes (kosher salt)

For the braised red cabbage

¼ red cabbage (approx. 200g/7oz), finely shredded

1 apple, peeled and cut into wedges

100ml (3½fl oz) vegetable stock

30ml (1fl oz) apple cider vinegar

20g (¾oz) caster (superfine) sugar

½ teaspoon ground cinnamon

2 star anise

1 bay leaf

For the vegetables

3 carrots, peeled and chopped into batons

100g (3½oz) frozen peas

To assemble

3 frozen Yorkshire pudding wraps (available from major supermarkets)

2 tablespoons horseradish sauce

600ml (20¼fl oz) beef gravy (or made from gravy granules of your choice)

First, prepare the roast potatoes. Warm the oil in a roasting tray (sheet pan) in the oven at 240°C/220°C fan/465°F/gas 9. Place a saucepan of salted water over a medium heat and bring to the boil. Add the potatoes and cook at a vigorous boil for 3 minutes. Drain the potatoes, tip them into the tray and toss in the hot oil.

Roast the potatoes in the hot oven for 15 minutes, then turn them, sprinkle over the salt and return to the oven for a further 10 minutes. Remove the tray from the oven, drain away any excess fat from the potatoes and set aside for later.

To prepare the cabbage, place all the ingredients in a saucepan over a medium heat and bring to the boil. Reduce the heat to low and leave to simmer for 20–30 minutes, stirring occasionally, until the cabbage is tender. You may need an extra splash of water to prevent the cabbage from sticking. Once cooked, remove the star anise and bay leaf, then set aside for later.

Over a medium heat, bring a saucepan of salted water to the boil. Add the carrots, reduce the heat to low and simmer for 8–10 minutes. Remove the carrots and set aside. Next, add the peas to the same saucepan briefly until thawed. Drain the peas and set aside for later.

If you are making this dish using leftovers, preheat the oven to 200°C/180°C fan/390°F/gas 6.

To assemble the lasagne, place a frozen Yorkshire pudding wrap or flattened Yorkshire pudding over the base of a 25 x 20-cm (10 x 8-inch) deep-sided ovenproof dish. Spread the Yorkshire pudding with 1 tablespoon horseradish sauce. Top with half of the roast beef slices. Next, add a layer of the cabbage and then the peas. Pour over 150ml (5½fl oz) gravy. Lay down a second Yorkshire pudding and spread that with another 1 tablespoon horseradish sauce. Top with the remainder of the roast beef slices. Spoon in the cauliflower cheese, including all the sauce, to cover the beef. Scatter over the carrots and pour over a further 150ml (5½fl oz) gravy. Finish with a third Yorkshire pudding, pour over a further 150ml (5½fl oz) gravy and then tumble over the roast potatoes.

Bake in the hot oven for 30 minutes or until the lasagne is bubbling. If the potatoes begin to take on too much colour, cover the tray with foil for the remaining cooking time.

Remove from the oven and allow to rest for 10 minutes before slicing and serving with the remainder of the gravy poured over.

CHICKEN QUESADILLA LASAGNE

This lasagne is a great midweek dinner to enjoy with friends. During my time at university, I often made this dish as it's packed with all the classic ingredients served with fajitas but with the added bonus of being made in one dish. Minimise washing up while maximising flavour. You can easily substitute tofu or aubergine (eggplant) for the chicken to make a vegetarian alternative.

Serves 3–4

2 tablespoons vegetable oil

1 onion, roughly chopped

2 red (bell) peppers, chopped into bite-size chunks

3 skinless, boneless chicken breasts, chopped into bite-size chunks

1 x 30-g (1-oz) sachet fajita seasoning mix (whichever flavour and heat level you prefer)

1 x 400-g (14-oz) can chopped tomatoes

1 x 400-g (14-oz) can refried beans

3–4 large tortilla wraps (depending on size)

150ml (5½fl oz) sour cream

200g (7oz) tomato salsa

150g (5½oz) Cheddar cheese or other mature hard cheese, grated (shredded)

2 ripe avocados, pitted, peeled and sliced lengthways

Heat the oil in a large frying pan (skillet) over a medium heat. Add the onion and peppers and cook for 5 minutes until softened. Add the chicken to the pan along with the fajita seasoning mix. Stir to combine and cook for a further 3 minutes or until the chicken is browned. Tip in the chopped tomatoes, then rinse the can with around 100ml (3½fl oz) cold water and add this to the pan. Simmer for a further 5 minutes, stirring occasionally, until the sauce has thickened.

Put the refried beans into a small saucepan and warm them over a low heat, adding a splash of cold water to loosen them. The beans do not need to be piping hot as they'll be going in the oven.

Preheat the oven to 200°C/180°C fan/390°F/gas 6.

Take a 20-cm (8-inch) round ovenproof dish or one that matches the size of your tortillas. Cover the base of the dish with the first tortilla. Spread 2–3 tablespoons of the sour cream over the tortilla, then half of the chicken before topping with half of the refried beans. Dollop 2 heaped tablespoons of the tomato salsa over the beans, then scatter 50g of cheese. Repeat these layers once more. Finish with a third tortilla wrap. Cover with the remaining sour cream, salsa and cheese.

Bake in the hot oven for 30–40 minutes or until piping hot all the way through and the cheese is gooey and melted. If the cheese is already browning but the lasagne isn't yet piping hot, cover the top with kitchen foil for the last 10 minutes of cooking. Remove the dish from the oven and allow the lasagne to cool for 5 minutes before slicing and serving. Serve with the sliced avocado.

LAMB, FETA AND FILO LASAGNE

Seasonal spring lamb mingles with salty feta and aromatic oregano and mint in this delightful dish, which is so full of flavour that it evokes memories of holidaying on a Greek island. I often feel lamb is an under-appreciated and under-used meat, so I've created a recipe to enjoy it as an alternative to the traditional roast, with buttery filo (phyllo) pastry instead of roast potatoes. If you have some to use up, you can always use minced (ground) beef instead of lamb – just be sure to use one with a high percentage of fat. Serve this lasagne with a refreshing green salad and a drizzle of tzatziki.

Serves 4

1 tablespoon vegetable oil

500g (1lb 2oz) minced (ground) lamb

1 large onion, roughly chopped

3 garlic cloves, roughly chopped

1 x 400-g (14-oz) can chopped tomatoes

2 teaspoons dried oregano

1 teaspoon ground cumin

1 teaspoon caster (superfine) sugar

75g (2½oz) feta cheese, crumbled

150g (5½oz) Greek yogurt

1 tablespoon milk

20g (¾oz) bunch of fresh mint, roughly chopped

3 tablespoons salted butter, melted

1 x 270-g (9½-oz) packet filo (phyllo) pastry, approx. 7 sheets

Heat the oil in a frying pan (skillet) over a medium heat. Add the minced lamb and fry for 2 minutes until browned, breaking up any clumps. Drain off any excess fat from the lamb. Add the onion and garlic and cook for a further 5 minutes until softened, stirring occasionally. Reduce the heat to low and stir in the chopped tomatoes. Rinse the can with 100ml (3½fl oz) cold water and add to this to the pan too. Finally, add the oregano, cumin and sugar and simmer for a further 8–10 minutes, or until the sauce has reduced. Remove the pan from the heat and stir in two-thirds of the feta.

In a separate bowl, mix together the yogurt, milk and mint. Stir to combine fully.

Preheat the oven to 200°C/180°C fan/390°F/gas 6.

Brush the base of a 25 x 20-cm (10 x 8-inch) ovenproof dish with a little melted butter. Fold one of the filo pastry sheets to make three layers. Trim it to the size of the dish, if necessary. Lay the folded filo pastry sheet over the base of the dish, brushing it with a little more melted butter before adding the next. (Keep the remaining pastry sheets covered when not in use to prevent them drying out.) Spread half of the lamb and feta mixture over the filo pastry and top with one-third of the minty yogurt. Repeat these layers once more, using two more filo pastry sheets. Finish with a third layer of filo pastry, using the last two sheets. Finally, cover the top pastry layer with the remaining yogurt and crumble over the last of the feta cheese.

Bake in the hot oven for 30 minutes, or until the pastry is golden and crispy. Cover the dish with foil and return to the oven for a further 15 minutes, or until the dish is bubbling but not burning.

Remove the dish from the oven and allow the lasagne to cool for 5 minutes before slicing and serving.

COOK'S TIP A 270-g (9½-oz) packet of filo (phyllo) pastry gives enough sheets for this dish. Any leftover sheets can be frozen to use later. Or why not make a sweet lasagne with tangy raspberries and a nutty chocolate spread layered between the filo pastry.

RAVIOLI LASAGNE

In this 'deconstructed' lasagne you have all the main components of a conventional lasagne – pasta, beef ragù, béchamel sauce, cheese – so it tastes just as delicious, even though it might not look as you'd expect. I've got a good friend to thank for the inspiration behind this recipe; he was devouring a bowlful of ravioli when I called in one day and the idea for this lasagne was born.

Serves 4

3 tablespoons vegetable oil

1 onion, finely chopped

2 garlic cloves, diced

3 thyme sprigs

4 smoked bacon rashers, chopped

300g (10½oz) courgette (zucchini), chopped into bite-size chunks

200g (7oz) red (bell) peppers, chopped into bite-size chunks

70g (2½oz) sundried tomatoes, roughly chopped

250ml (9fl oz) red wine

400ml (14fl oz) tomato passata (strained tomatoes)

30g (1oz) salted butter

30g (1oz) plain (all-purpose) flour

330ml (11fl oz) milk

2 x 250-g (9-oz) packets ravioli stuffed with beef ragù

50g (1¾oz) Parmesan cheese, grated (shredded)

Salt and freshly ground black pepper

In a large frying pan (skillet), heat the oil over a medium heat. Add the onion, garlic and thyme and cook, stirring, for 3 minutes. Add the bacon and fry for a further 2 minutes. Add the courgette, red peppers and sundried tomatoes and cook for a further 5 minutes until the vegetables have softened a little. Next, pour in the red wine and tomato passata. Simmer for 20–25 minutes until the sauce has reduced and thickened.

Combine the butter and flour in a saucepan over a low heat. Stir to make a roux before gradually adding the milk, stirring continuously so lumps do not form. Season with salt and pepper.

Preheat the oven to 200°C/180°C fan/390°F/gas 6.

Cover a 25 x 20-cm (10 x 8-inch) ovenproof dish with a layer of the fresh pasta ravioli. Top with half of the tomato sauce and then one-third of the béchamel sauce. Repeat these steps once more, finishing with a third layer of ravioli and top with the remainder of the béchamel sauce. Scatter over the Parmesan.

Bake in the preheated oven for 25–30 minutes until the lasagne is bubbling and the cheese has melted. Remove the dish from the oven and set aside the lasagne for 2 minutes before serving.

COOK'S TIP Use fresh pasta ravioli in any flavour you fancy, whether that be Porcini mushroom and truffle, or spinach and ricotta. Just make sure you get the flat, pillow-shaped ravioli and not button-shaped tortellini. You can even substitute the fresh pasta ravioli for a can of ravioli pasta. While the canned ravioli might be a little smaller, they work perfectly well as a layer.

LOADED DIRTY BURGER LASAGNE

The name of this lasagne tells you all you need to know: it's delicious, it's dirty and it's delightfully naughty. I promise you'll be sneaking back for seconds. I based this dish on the classic American-diner burger and fries, but then added macaroni cheese and crispy fried onions – the surprise stars of this showstopper, which really make the dish stratospheric.

Serves 4–6

For the macaroni cheese

200g (7oz) dried macaroni

50g (1¾oz) salted butter

50g (1¾oz) plain (all-purpose) flour

500ml (17fl oz) milk

50g (1¾oz) Cheddar cheese

For the ricotta sauce

250g (9oz) ricotta cheese

75g (2½oz) burger sauce (available from major supermarkets)

3–4 tablespoons milk

For the burgers

4 beef burgers, halved across the middle to create 8 rounds

8 burger cheese slices

To assemble

8 streaky bacon rashers

1 tablespoon oil

1 onion, finely sliced

100g (3½oz) pickled gherkins, thinly sliced

First, make the macaroni cheese. Bring a saucepan of water to the boil, add the macaroni and cook until al dente (usually a few minutes less than stated on the packet). Drain and set aside.

Meanwhile, in a separate saucepan over a low heat, melt the butter. Add the flour and stir to combine. Slowly pour in the milk, stirring continuously to thicken the sauce. Next, add the grated cheese and then stir in the cooked pasta. Remove the pan from the heat and set aside.

To make the ricotta sauce, combine the ricotta, burger sauce and milk in a bowl. Stir to mix everything well and set aside.

Place a large frying pan (skillet) over a medium heat. Place the burger rounds in the dry pan to cook for 2 minutes on each side to brown the meat. The burgers don't need to be cooked through as this will happen in the oven. Transfer the burgers to a roasting tray (sheet pan) and top each one with a cheese slice.

Wipe out the frying pan, then fry the bacon, flipping occasionally, until golden and crispy on both sides. Roughly chop and set aside.

Heat the oil in the frying pan, add the sliced onion and sauté for 10–12 minutes or until brown. Transfer to a plate and set aside.

Preheat the oven to 200°C/180°C fan/390°F/gas 6.

Cover the base of a 30-cm (12-inch) deep-sided ovenproof dish with half of the macaroni cheese. Top with 4 cheesed burgers, followed by half of the bacon, crispy fried onions, gherkins and tomato slices. Next, pour over the remaining macaroni cheese and

2 salad tomatoes, sliced

300g (10½oz) frozen slim-cut oven fries

1 teaspoon coarse sea salt flakes

Tomato ketchup

Mild yellow mustard

then lay the remaining 4 cheesed burgers over the macaroni followed by the rest of the toppings. Cover everything with the ricotta sauce. Lastly, arrange the frozen fries on top and sprinkle over the salt.

Bake in the hot oven for 25–30 minutes or until the lasagne is cooked through and the fries are golden and crispy.

Remove from the oven and allow to rest for 10 minutes before serving. Drizzle over plenty of tomato ketchup and squeezy yellow mustard.

FISH & SEAFOOD

PRAWN, CHICKEN AND CHORIZO TRAYBAKE

This traybake takes inspiration from a traditional jambalaya, but it's served in a slightly different way with layers of rice between the gorgeous prawns (shrimp) and chicken which burst with flavour from the smoked paprika and sweet red (bell) peppers. With simple and time-saving tricks, I promise this dish will become a favourite speedy midweek meal.

Serves 6

2 tablespoons vegetable oil

1 onion, finely chopped

2 garlic cloves, diced

2 sweet pointed red (bell) peppers, chopped into bite-size chunks

2 large skinless, boneless chicken thighs, cut into bite-size chunks

150g (5½oz) chorizo, roughly sliced

2 teaspoons smoked paprika

1 chicken stock cube, dissolved in 100ml (3½fl oz) boiling water

1 x 400-g (14-oz) can chopped tomatoes

200g (7oz) raw king prawns (jumbo shrimp)

3 x 250-g (9-oz) pouches microwaveable brown basmati and wild rice

To serve

Chopped parsley

Lemon wedges

Crisp green salad

Preheat the oven to 200°C/180°C fan/390°F/gas 6.

Place the oil in a large frying pan (skillet) over a medium heat. Add the onion and fry gently for 10 minutes or until translucent. Add the garlic and peppers, then continue cooking until the peppers have softened. Next, add the chicken and cook for 3 minutes or until browned all over. Add the chorizo and sprinkle in the paprika. Stir to combine and cook for a further few minutes.

Pour in the stock and chopped tomatoes. Bring to the boil and then reduce the heat and simmer for 15 minutes, stirring occasionally. If the mixture is sticking to the bottom of the pan, add a splash of cold water. Remove the pan from the heat and stir through the prawns.

Cover the base of a 25 x 20-cm (10 x 8-inch) ovenproof dish with one pouch of rice. Top with half of the prawn and chicken mixture.

Repeat the layers of rice and prawn and chicken mixture once more. Finish with a third layer of rice.

Cover the dish with foil and place in the hot oven for 20 minutes or until the traybake is piping hot throughout. Remove the foil and bake for a further 10 minutes.

Remove the dish from the oven and allow the traybake to cool for 2 minutes before scattering over the parsley. Serve with lemon wedges for squeezing over and a crisp green salad on the side.

FISH AND CHIPS LASAGNE

A twist on the British seaside favourite, this holds all the delights of a 'fish supper' and can be enjoyed in one mouthful. Potato rösti is an underrated way to enjoy the classic spud and works perfectly as the layer. If time is tight, you can use oven chips instead – just par-cook them prior to assembly. The inclusion of mushy peas not only adds to the novelty factor, it also brings a sweet and fresh taste.

Serves 4

For the potato rösti

8 medium Maris Piper potatoes (approx. 1.3kg/ 2lb 14oz), peeled

1 onion, finely sliced

2 tablespoons plain (all-purpose) flour

6 tablespoons vegetable oil

Salt and freshly ground black pepper

For the fish

4 haddock fillets or other firm white fish (approx. 400g/14oz), chopped into bite-size chunks

500g (1lb 2oz) ricotta cheese

100ml (3½fl oz) milk

3 heaped tablespoons tartare sauce

To assemble

1 x 300-g (10½-oz) can mushy peas

To serve

Lemon wedges

Tomato ketchup

To make the rösti, coarsely grate the potatoes into a clean dish towel. Fold and squeeze to remove as much moisture as possible. Transfer the grated potato to a bowl. Stir in the onion and flour, then season with plenty of salt and pepper.

Heat 2 tablespoons oil in a large frying pan (skillet) over a medium heat. Spoon one-third of the potato into the pan and mould into a 1cm (⅓ inch) thick round the same size as your baking dish. I use a 20-cm (8-inch) deep-sided ovenproof dish. Fry the rösti for 3 minutes, then flip over and cook for a further 3 minutes on the other side. The rösti should be crispy and golden on both sides. Transfer the rösti to kitchen paper. Repeat this twice more with the rest of the potato, adding more oil each time. Set aside the rösti.

Put the pan back on a medium heat. Add the haddock and cook for 2 minutes, stirring. Remove the pan from the heat and set aside.

In a bowl, combine the ricotta, milk and tartare sauce. Season well with salt and pepper. Stir the haddock into the sauce.

Preheat the oven to 200°C/180°C fan/390°F/gas 6.

Cover the base of your dish with a rösti. Spoon over half of the fish mixture, then top with half of the peas. Repeat these layers once more. Finish with the third rösti.

Bake in the hot oven for 30–40 minutes or until the lasagne is bubbling and the top is crispy and golden.

Remove the dish from the oven and allow the lasagne to cool for a few minutes before serving. Serve sprinkled with salt, with wedges of lemon for squeezing over and plenty of ketchup. Or for the real chip-shop experience, drenched in malt vinegar with a pickled egg.

COOK'S TIP A round ovenproof dish is the best choice here as the rösti are fried in a frying pan, but you can play around with the shape and size when moulding the potato to suit your dish.

SALMON AND PAK CHOI LASAGNE

This dish bursts with the characteristic umami of soy sauce balanced by the creaminess of cashews. Salmon works wonderfully well in carrying this breadth of flavours, but you could easily substitute it for trout. Cashew nut butter was an incredible discovery while developing this recipe; it's as versatile as other nut butters but has that extra richness, making it a superb base ingredient for a sauce.

Serves 4

500g (1lb 2oz) salmon fillets, skinned and chopped into bite-size chunks

5 tablespoons dark soy sauce

2 tablespoons vegetable oil

1 onion, finely diced

3 garlic cloves, finely diced

250g (9oz) broccoli, chopped into bite-size pieces

3 pak choi

125g (4½oz) cashew butter

100ml (3½fl oz) milk

25g (¾oz) unsalted cashew nuts, roughly chopped

1 large baguette, sliced

Place the salmon chunks in a bowl with 3 tablespoons soy sauce. Leave to marinate for at least 30 minutes, or preferably longer.

Preheat the oven to 200°C/180°C fan/390°F/gas 6.

Heat the oil in a frying pan (skillet) over a medium heat. Cook the onion and garlic for 3 minutes. Add the broccoli pieces and cook for a further 3 minutes or until the broccoli is slightly charred.

Trim the base from each pak choi so the leaves separate. Set aside the largest leaves for layering the lasagne, then chop the central hearts into thin slices. Add the sliced pak choi to the pan and cook for 3 minutes. Finally, add the marinated salmon and the remaining soy sauce. Reduce the heat to low and allow the salmon to brown gently for a few minutes. Remove the pan from the heat.

Add the cashew butter to a separate pan over a low heat, and slowly pour in the milk with 100ml (3½fl oz) water. Cook, stirring continuously to create a pouring sauce. Add all but 3 tablespoons of the cashew sauce to the salmon and stir to combine.

Cover the base of a 25 x 20-cm (10 x 8-inch) ovenproof dish with a layer of pak choi. Spread over half the salmon and cashew mixture. Top with a second layer of pak choi, then cover with the remaining salmon and cashew mixture. Top with a third layer of pak choi. Finish by spooning over the reserved cashew sauce.

Cover the dish with foil and bake in the hot oven for 20 minutes. Remove the foil, scatter over the cashews and return to the oven for 10 minutes or until the pak choi are softened and the nuts are crisp. Remove from the oven and allow to cool for 5 minutes before serving with hunks of baguette to soak up the nutty sauce.

SATAY PRAWN NOODLE LASAGNE

Whip up this saucy lasagne in an evening to make the perfect midweek meal. I took inspiration from the classic spring roll with crispy rice papers forming the layers, a fresh and crunchy noodle stir-fry making up the body of the lasagne and finally a delightfully rich and nutty satay sauce oozing throughout. The prawns (shrimp) can easily be substituted for tofu, if you prefer a veggie lasagne.

Serves 6

3 tablespoons vegetable oil

1 sweetheart cabbage (approx. 500g/1lb 2oz), finely shredded

5 spring onions (scallions), roughly chopped

200g (7oz) mangetout (snow peas), sliced into thirds

250g (9oz) ready-to-cook ribbon rice noodles

300g (10½oz) peeled raw king prawns (jumbo shrimp)

200g (7oz) unsweetened peanut butter (smooth or crunchy)

4 tablespoons sweet chilli sauce

4 tablespoons dark soy sauce

1 x 400-ml (14fl-oz) can coconut milk

10–12 rice paper sheets

To serve

Bunch of fresh coriander (cilantro)

1 lime, cut into wedges

Preheat the oven to 200°C/180°C fan/390°F/gas 6.

Heat 1 tablespoon oil in a frying pan (skillet) over a medium heat. Stir-fry the cabbage until wilted, then transfer to a bowl. Add the spring onions and mangetout and stir-fry until just cooked. Mix in the noodles with a splash of water, then transfer to the bowl. Add 1 tablespoon oil to the pan and stir-fry the prawns for 2 minutes or until they just turn pink. Transfer to the bowl and set aside.

Combine the peanut butter, sweet chilli sauce and soy sauce in a pan over a low heat. Gradually stir in the coconut milk. Simmer for 2–3 minutes, stirring occasionally, until slightly thickened. Remove from the heat and pour the satay sauce over the stir-fry in the bowl, toss all the ingredients until fully coated in the sauce.

When ready to assemble, prepare the rice paper. Soak the sheets individually in warm water for 5 seconds before blotting dry with a clean dish towel. Use the rice paper sheets immediately while malleable and they can be made to fit your baking dish.

Drizzle 2 teaspoons vegetable oil over the base of a 25 x 20-cm (10 x 8-inch) ovenproof dish. Cover the base of the dish with a layer of prepared rice paper. The sheets are delicate, so overlap them slightly for maximum stability. Spoon over half of the satay prawn mixture. Repeat these layers once more. Finish with a third layer of rice paper. Brush the top with the remaining oil.

Bake in the hot oven for 20 minutes or until the top is golden and crispy and the lasagne is bubbling. Set aside for 10 minutes before slicing and serving with a handful of coriander and lime wedges.

CURRIED COD AND CAULIFLOWER BAKE

This hearty meal makes a delicious change to your family's favourite curry. The combination of gently spiced cod and cauliflower is perfect for an autumnal midweek supper. If responsibly sourced cod is unavailable, substitute another firm white fish, such as haddock or hake. Enjoy this unique bake with stir-fried kale or seasonal greens tossed with chilli flakes for a little extra warmth.

Serves 4

2 tablespoons coconut oil

1 onion, finely chopped

2 teaspoons ground turmeric

1 cauliflower, leaves and stalk removed and florets chopped into bite-size pieces

400g (14oz) cod fillets, or any other firm white fish, cut into bite-size chunks

2 x 70-g (2½-oz) curry paste pots (whichever strength you prefer)

1 x 400-ml (14fl-oz) can coconut milk

4–5 large potatoes, such as Maris Piper

Salt and freshly ground black pepper

Heat the oil in a frying pan (skillet) over a medium heat. Add the onion and cook for 3 minutes or until softened. Add the turmeric and cook, stirring, for a further 1 minute. Reduce the heat to low, add the cauliflower and cook for 10 minutes or until slightly softened. Add a splash of water to the pan and stir in the cod chunks before adding the curry paste and coconut milk. Stir again to combine well and simmer over a low heat for 10 minutes or until the fish is cooked through. Season to taste. Remove from the heat and set aside the curry mixture until needed.

Meanwhile, carefully cut the potatoes into 2-mm (1/16-inch) slices. Either use a mandoline or a very sharp knife to cut the potato slices as thinly as possible.

Preheat the oven to 180°C/160°C fan/350°F/gas 4.

Cover the base of a 25 x 20-cm (10 x 8-inch) ovenproof dish with a layer of the potato slices. Measure out 4 tablespoons of sauce from the curry mixture and set aside. Spoon half of the curried cod and cauliflower over the potato layer. Repeat these layers once more, then top with a third and final layer of potato slices. Finally, cover the top potato layer with the reserved curry sauce.

Bake in the hot oven for 45–50 minutes or until the potatoes are soft – test by piercing through the entire depth of the dish with a sharp knife. The top layer of potato should be golden and crispy.

Remove the dish from the oven and allow the bake to cool for 5 minutes before serving.

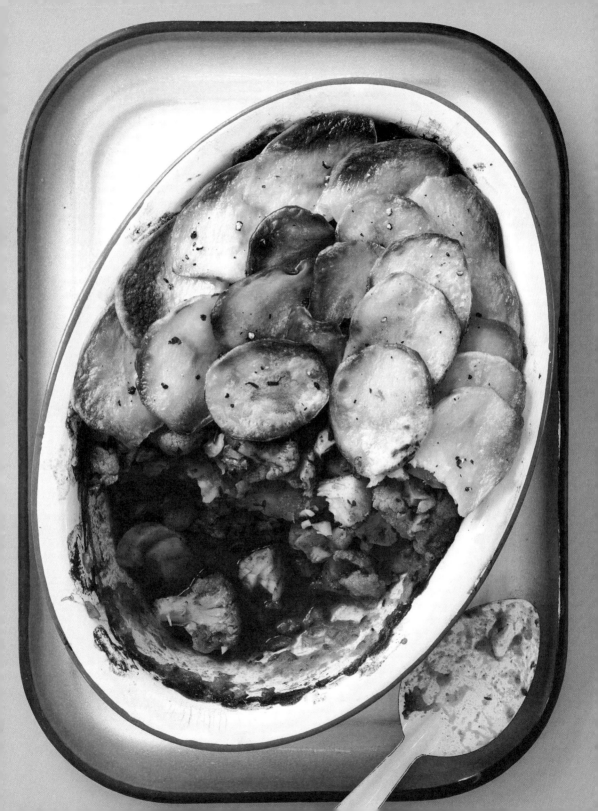

COD AND PARMA HAM LASAGNE

This decadent lasagne is a delightful weekend treat. Cod is rather robust and so works wonderfully in this recipe and carries the creamy mascarpone and rich red wine exceptionally well. Using Parma ham as the 'layer' is an ingenious way of incorporating more flavour into this lasagne.

Serves 6

2 tablespoons olive oil

1 onion, finely chopped

3 garlic cloves, grated or crushed

200ml (7fl oz) red wine

350g (12½oz) cherry tomatoes, halved

500ml (17fl oz) tomato passata (strained tomatoes)

200g (7oz) fresh spinach

600g (1lb 5oz) cod (or hake or any other firm white fish), chopped into bite-size chunks

250g (9oz) mascarpone cheese

150g (5½oz) giant couscous

1 vegetable stock cube

12 Parma ham slices

Bunch of basil leaves

Preheat the oven to 200°C/180°C fan/390°F/gas 6.

Heat the oil in a large frying pan (skillet) over a medium heat. Add the onion and garlic with a pinch of salt and cook for 5 minutes until softened. Add the wine and simmer over a high heat for a further 5 minutes or until the wine has reduced. Add the cherry tomatoes and tomato passata and simmer for a further 15 minutes. Scoop a few ladlefuls of the sauce into a bowl and set aside for later.

Stir the spinach and cod into the sauce and cook for a further 2 minutes. Remove from the heat and stir in the mascarpone.

Meanwhile, cook the couscous according to the instructions on the packet, adding the stock cube to the water. Once the couscous is cooked, drain through a sieve (strainer) to remove any excess moisture. Tip the cooked couscous into the cod mixture and stir thoroughly to combine.

Spoon the reserved sauce into a 25 x 20-cm (10 x 8-inch) ovenproof dish. Arrange a layer of Parma ham slices over the sauce, then spread over half of the cod and couscous mixture. Repeat the layers once more. Finish with a third layer of Parma ham slices.

Cover the dish with foil and bake in the hot oven for 20 minutes or until cooked through. Remove the foil and cook for a further 5 minutes to crisp up the top layer. Remove the dish from the oven and allow the lasagne to cool for a few minutes. Scatter over a handful of basil leaves before serving.

COOK'S TIP Instead of couscous you can use quinoa or lentils; the microwave pouches work perfectly as an alternative.

PESTO SALMON AND ASPARAGUS LASAGNE

Making this lasagne, you don't need to use the expensive fillets of fish; instead the cheaper salmon pieces often sold for making a fish pie work perfectly. The stems of the asparagus spears and stalks of the broccoli are just as tasty and nutritious as the tips and florets; chuck them in too so that nothing is wasted. This lasagne is simple to make and healthy to eat – excellent for a quick supper, with leftovers for lunch the next day!

Serves 4

2 tablespoons vegetable oil

200g (7oz) Tenderstem broccoli, florets and stalk chopped into bite-size chunks

250g (9oz) asparagus spears, stems trimmed and chopped into bite-size chunks

300ml (10½fl oz) crème fraîche

160g (5½oz) basil pesto

450g (1lb) salmon pieces, skinned and chopped into bite-size chunks

2 tablespoons milk (if needed)

4–6 fresh pasta lasagne sheets

30g (1oz) Parmesan cheese, grated (shredded)

Heat the oil in a large frying pan over a medium heat. Add the broccoli and asparagus to the pan and cook for 3 minutes until lightly browned. Reduce the heat to low and add 270ml (9fl oz) of the crème fraîche and 140g (5oz) of the pesto, reserving the rest for later. Stir to combine and simmer for 5 minutes until the sauce has thickened and is glossy.

Add the salmon pieces and stir to fully coat with the sauce and simmer for 5 minutes. You may not need it, but if the sauce is too thick add a splash of milk but no more than 2 tablespoons. The salmon pieces might flake in the sauce, which is fine.

Preheat the oven to 200°C/180°C fan/390°F/gas 6.

Cover the base of a 25 x 20-cm (10 x 8-inch) ovenproof dish with one of the lasagne sheets, cutting the sheet to fit your dish. Spoon over half the pesto salmon. Repeat the above steps once more, finishing with a third layer of lasagne sheets.

In a small bowl, combine the remaining crème fraîche and pesto, then spread this over the top of the lasagne sheet. Scatter over the Parmesan.

Bake in the hot oven for 30 minutes or until the lasagne is bubbling and the cheese has melted. Remove from the oven and let the lasagne cool for a few minutes before slicing and serving.

TERIYAKI SALMON LASAGNE WITH COURGETTE AND QUINOA

The sweet, tangy teriyaki provides a wonderful backdrop of flavours that unifies the salmon, vegetables and grains so effortlessly. This simple, speedy lasagne can be rustled up and on your plate in under an hour, providing an easy midweek dinner that also happens to be super healthy.

Serves 4

2 tablespoons vegetable oil

150g (5½oz) baby corn, chopped into bite-size pieces

1 x 250-g (9-oz) pouch ready-cooked quinoa

250g (9oz) teriyaki sauce

300ml (10½fl oz) fish stock

400g (14oz) salmon pieces, skinned and chopped into bite-size chunks

300g (10½oz) crème fraîche

30g (1oz) tahini

Juice of 1 lemon

3 courgettes (zucchini), very thinly sliced lengthways into 2-mm (¹⁄₁₆-inch) thick ribbons

150g (5½oz) sugar snap peas, trimmed and halved

25g (¾oz) sesame seeds

Salt and freshly ground black pepper

Preheat the oven to 200°C/180°C fan/390°F/gas 6.

Warm the oil in a large frying pan (skillet) over a medium heat. Add the baby corn and gently cook for 3 minutes. Then add the quinoa and stir to combine. Reduce the heat to low and add the teriyaki sauce, stirring into the mixture. Gradually pour in the stock and simmer for 15 minutes, until the liquid has reduced and the sauce has thickened.

Remove from the heat and stir in the salmon pieces. Don't worry if it flakes through the quinoa and vegetables. Set aside for later.

In a separate bowl, combine the crème fraîche and tahini to form a thick sauce. Gradually stir in the lemon juice and season well. If needed, add a splash of water to thin the sauce a little more.

Cover the base of a 25 x 20-cm (10 x 8-inch) ovenproof dish with a layer of courgette ribbons. Spoon half of the salmon and quinoa mixture over the courgettes, scatter over half of the sugar snaps, then top with one-third of the tahini crème fraîche. Repeat the layers once more. Finish with a third layer of courgette ribbons. Lastly, top with the remaining tahini crème fraîche.

Cover the dish with foil and bake in the hot oven for 20 minutes. Remove and sprinkle the sesame seeds over then return to the oven for a further 5–10 minutes until the lasagne is bubbling.

Remove the dish from the oven and leave the lasagne to settle for a few minutes before slicing and serving.

HALIBUT, MANGO AND COCONUT LASAGNE

This is a rather luxurious lasagne, yet utterly simple to make. I have to admit it is an ultra-indulgent recipe but one that I'm sure you'll fall in love with. The meaty halibut is sublime with the sweet mango, while the fragrant Thai flavours pierce through the creamy coconut, making a rather hot and silky dish. This lasagne is one to serve if you want to impress.

Serves 6

1 x 400-ml (14fl-oz) can coconut milk

170g (6oz) Thai red curry paste

1 large firm mango, peeled, pitted and chopped into bite-size chunks

450g (1lb) halibut fillet or any other firm white fish, chopped into bite-size chunks

300g (10½oz) crème fraîche

100g (3½oz) mango chutney

Juice of 1 lime

9–10 fresh lasagne sheets

30g (1oz) unsweetened desiccated coconut

Preheat the oven to 200°C/180°C fan/390°F/gas 6.

Place a saucepan over a medium heat. Pour in the coconut milk and bring to a boil. Add the curry paste and boil for 10–15 minutes, stirring occasionally, until the sauce has thickened and is glossy.

Reduce the heat to low, add the mango chunks and stir. Simmer for 2 minutes, then stir through the halibut chunks and stir again. Immediately remove the pan from the heat as the fish doesn't need to cook at this stage.

In a separate bowl, combine the crème fraîche, mango chutney and lime juice. Stir until fully mixed.

Cover the base of a 25 x 20-cm (10 x 8-inch) ovenproof dish with a layer of lasagne sheets. Trim them to fit the dish, if necessary. Spoon over half of the halibut mixture and top with one-third of the crème fraîche sauce. Repeat these layers once more. Finish with a third layer of lasagne sheets. Finally, top with the remaining crème fraîche sauce and scatter over the desiccated coconut.

Place the dish in the oven and bake the lasagne for 30 minutes or until the top is golden and the lasagne is bubbling.

Remove the dish from the oven and allow the lasagne to cool for 10 minutes before slicing and serving.

COOK'S TIP If halibut isn't easy to source, you can easily substitute it for any other firm white fish, such as hake, haddock or cod, or even prawns.

HARISSA TUNA LASAGNE

This lasagne is full of rich flavours. Using canned tuna and lentils is a time-saving and cost-cutting hack with minimal effort required. If you prefer, swap the tuna for chickpeas (garbanzo beans) for a veggie lasagne.

Serves 6

2 tablespoons vegetable oil

1 onion, finely chopped

2 carrots, peeled and diced into 6-mm (¼-inch) cubes

2 celery sticks, diced into 6-mm (¼-inch) cubes

3 garlic cloves, finely diced

2 teaspoons dried mixed herbs

1 stock pot (vegetable or fish)

500g (1lb 2oz) tomato passata (strained tomatoes)

1 tablespoon Worcestershire sauce

1 tablespoon tomato ketchup

1 x 400-g (14-oz) can green lentils, drained

2 x 145-g (5-oz) cans tuna in spring water, drained

200g (7oz) fresh spinach

300g (10½oz) crème fraîche

100ml (3½fl oz) double (heavy) cream

75g (2½oz) harissa paste

9–12 dried lasagne sheets

50g (1¾oz) Parmesan cheese, grated (shredded)

Salt and freshly ground black pepper

Preheat the oven to 200°C/180°C fan/390°F/gas 6.

Warm the oil in a large frying pan (skillet) over a medium heat. Add the onion, carrot and celery and cook for 10 minutes, stirring occasionally, until the vegetables have softened. Add the garlic and mixed herbs and cook for a further 2 minutes.

Add the stock pot and then pour in the tomato passata. Finally, stir in the Worcestershire sauce and tomato ketchup. Season well with salt and pepper. Once bubbling, reduce the heat to low and simmer for 10–15 minutes or until the sauce has thickened.

Stir the lentils and tuna into the tomato sauce. Simmer on a low heat for 2 minutes or until fully combined. In the last minute, gradually stir in the spinach leaves so they wilt into the mixture. Remove the pan from the heat and set aside.

In a separate bowl, combine the crème fraîche, cream and harissa paste. Stir to fully combine and set aside.

Cover the base of a 25 x 20-cm (10 x 8-inch) ovenproof dish with a layer of lasagne sheets. You may need to snap them to fit. Top with half of the tuna and lentil mixture and then spread over one-third of the crème fraîche sauce. Repeat the layers once more. Finish with a third layer of pasta sheets, then spread over a thick covering of the remaining sauce and sprinkle over the Parmesan.

Bake the lasagne in the hot oven for 15 minutes or until the cheese has melted. Cover the dish with foil and cook for a further 40–45 minutes or until the lasagne is bubbling.

Remove the dish from the oven and allow to rest for 10 minutes before slicing and serving.

VEGETARIAN
& VEGAN

BEETROOT, BUTTERNUT AND PECAN LASAGNE

A lovely autumnal lasagne, this dish both looks and tastes sensational. The vibrant colours from the vegetables combine with the crunch from the nuts to make this recipe really appetising. The inclusion of goats' cheese adds a subtle extra hint of creaminess to this rather classic sauce.

Serves 6

1 butternut squash (1.5kg/ 3lb 5oz), peeled and chopped into bite-size chunks

4 large beetroot (beets), peeled and chopped into bite-size chunks

3 tablespoons olive oil

2 teaspoons smoked paprika

6 thyme sprigs

100g (3½oz) pecans

50g (1¾oz) butter

50g (1¾oz) plain (all-purpose) flour

500–600ml (17–20¼fl oz) milk

200g (7oz) vegetarian soft goats' cheese, rind removed

200g (7oz) fresh spinach

9–12 fresh lasagne sheets

Salt and freshly ground black pepper

Preheat the oven to 220°C/200°C fan/430°F/gas 7.

Place the butternut squash and beetroot chunks in a roasting tray (sheet pan) and drizzle over the oil, sprinkle with the paprika and add the thyme sprigs. Season well with salt and pepper, then toss the vegetables in the tray until fully coated.

Roast the vegetables in the hot oven for 45 minutes or so, shaking the tray halfway through the cooking time to turn the vegetables over. Remove from the oven, drain off any excess oil from the tray and removing any hard thyme stalks, then set aside.

Put the pecans on another roasting tray and gently toast in the oven for 10 minutes until fragrant. Remove from the oven and allow the lasagne to cool before roughly chopping.

Lower the oven temperature to 200°C/180°C fan/390°F/gas 6.

Melt the butter in a saucepan over a low heat. Stirring continuously, add the flour until combined. Gradually whisk in 500ml (17fl oz) milk until there are no lumps and the sauce has thickened. Stir 160g (5½oz) of the goats' cheese into the sauce until fully melted. Season to taste with salt and pepper. Remove from the heat. If the sauce appears a little too thick, add up to another 100ml (3½fl oz) milk to loosen it. Transfer one-third of the sauce to a bowl and set aside. Add the roasted vegetables and most of the pecans to the two-thirds of the sauce left in the pan.

Cover the base of a 25 x 20-cm (10 x 8-inch) ovenproof dish with a layer of lasagne sheets. Spoon over half of the roasted vegetables and pecans in the sauce. Top with half of the fresh spinach.

Repeat these layers once more, pushing the lasagne sheets down to compact the spinach leaves beneath. Finish with a third layer of lasagne sheets, then top with the reserved cheesy sauce from the bowl. Dot the remaining goats' cheese over the top.

Place the ovenproof dish on a baking tray and bake in the hot oven for 15 minutes or until the goats' cheese has melted. Cover the dish with foil and return to the oven for a further 40–45 minutes or until the lasagne is cooked through.

Remove the dish from the oven and allow to rest for 10 minutes before scattering over the remaining chopped pecans, then slicing and serving.

COOK'S TIP Sometimes when I make this dish, I add a rather unconventional topping at the end of assembling the lasagne: crumbled sour cream and chive Pringles. I must credit a close friend for this idea who – through his love of the culinary queen (Nigella) – inspired this ingenious optional addition.

POLENTA, PEPPER AND PEANUT LASAGNE

You're in for a tasty and unexpected surprise with this vegetarian lasagne. Let me reintroduce you to an often forgotten ingredient – polenta. Here it works wonderfully well with the scrumptious Mediterranean flavours. The addition of chilli flakes and cheese to the polenta elevates the flavours in the layers. My unconventional take on the classic béchamel sauce is a welcome kitchen shortcut.

Serves 4

For the polenta

2 vegetable stock pots or
3–4 stock cubes

160g (5½oz) instant polenta
(precooked ground maize)

1 teaspoon chilli flakes

75g (2½oz) vegan applewood
smoked cheese, grated
(shredded)

Salt and freshly ground
black pepper

For the peppers

2 tablespoons olive oil

1 teaspoon garlic paste

2 teaspoons dried basil

2 yellow (bell) peppers,
chopped into bite-size pieces

100g (3½oz) sundried
tomatoes

1 x 240-g (8½-oz) can
cannellini (white kidney) beans

2 tablespoons tomato paste
(concentrated purée)

1 x 400-g (14-oz) can chopped
tomatoes

Put the stock pots or cubes in a saucepan and pour in 800ml (27fl oz) water. Bring to the boil, then immediately add the polenta. Whisk continuously for 5 minutes or until thickened. Stir in the chilli flakes and 25g (¾oz) applewood smoked cheese and season with salt and pepper.

Line three 25 x 20-cm (10 x 8-inch) roasting trays (sheet pans) with parchment paper. Divide the polenta mixture evenly between the three lined trays. Spread out the polenta to no more than 1cm (⅓ inch) thick. (If you don't have three individual roasting trays, pour the polenta into one or two larger trays to set and then trim the polenta slabs to the required size once it has set.) Place the polenta in the fridge to set for at least 2 hours.

In a frying pan (skillet), heat the oil. Add the garlic paste and dried basil to the pan. Cook while stirring for 1 minute before adding the yellow peppers. Cook for 5 minutes until the peppers are slightly softened. Add the sundried tomatoes and cannellini beans before stirring in the tomato paste.

Next, add the chopped tomatoes. Rinse the can with around 100ml (3½fl oz) water and pour this into the pan. Season with salt and pepper and simmer for 15 minutes or until the sauce has thickened and is glossy.

Continued overleaf

For the peanut sauce

60g (2oz) unsweetened peanut butter (crunchy or smooth)

350ml (12fl oz) milk

15g (½oz) cornflour (cornstarch), mixed with 1 teaspoon cold water (optional)

Place the peanut butter and milk in a heavy-based saucepan and stir continuously over a low heat until combined. The peanut sauce should be of a pouring consistency. If it's too runny, add a little of the cornflour mixture.

Preheat the oven to 200°C/180°C fan/390°F/gas 6.

Drizzle 1 teaspoon oil over the base of a 25 x 20-cm (10 x 8-inch) ovenproof dish. Lay one of the polenta slabs in the dish to cover the base. Top with half the pepper mixture and then one-third of the peanut sauce. Repeat these layers once more. Finish with the final slab of polenta and the remaining peanut sauce. Sprinkle over the remaining applewood smoked cheese.

Place the dish on a baking sheet and bake in the hot oven for 15–20 minutes or until the cheese has melted and the lasagne is bubbling.

Remove the dish from the oven and allow the lasagne to cool for 5 minutes before slicing and serving.

COOK'S TIP Use alternative nut butters, such as cashew or almond, to make my easy version of a béchamel sauce. Also, you can use a plant-based milk, such as oat or soy, to make this dish vegan. Just make sure both the nut butter and milk you use are unsweetened. The nutty notes of the applewood smoked cheese complement the other flavours in this lasagne, but you can substitute your favourite vegan cheese alternative.

VEGAN MIXED BEAN AND RATATOUILLE LASAGNE

Ratatouille is a universally loved and truly comforting dish, so I've taken the key ingredients of this vegetable stew and made a nutritious and nourishing lasagne. The warmth from the chilli really packs a punch with this colourful vegetable medley, while the buttery texture of the beans will have even the most ardent meat-eater fooled – this recipe is 100% vegan.

Serves 6

6 tablespoons olive oil

1 red onion, cut into wedges

3 garlic cloves, diced

1 red chilli, deseeded and finely sliced

Large handful of basil leaves, chopped

2 yellow (bell) peppers, chopped into 3-cm (1-inch) chunks

1 courgette (zucchini), chopped into 3-cm (1-inch) chunks

4 tomatoes, cut into wedges

2 x 270-g (9½-oz) cans mixed beans in water

2 x 400-g (14-oz) cans chopped tomatoes

350g (12½oz) tomato passata (strained tomatoes)

1½ tablespoons balsamic vinegar

2 teaspoons caster (superfine) sugar

Preheat the oven to 200°C/180°C fan/390°F/gas 6.

Heat 2 tablespoons oil in a large frying pan (skillet) over a medium heat. Add the onion, garlic, chilli and most of the basil, reserving a few leaves for later. Cook for 5 minutes, then add the yellow peppers and courgette and cook for a further 10 minutes or until softened and browned. Add the fresh tomatoes and season well with salt and pepper.

Drain the mixed beans. Reduce the heat to low and add the mixed beans, chopped tomatoes and tomato passata. Rinse out the tomato can with 30ml (1fl oz) cold water and add to the pan. Stir well to make sure everything is combined before adding the vinegar and sugar. Simmer for 30 minutes until the ratatouille has thickened. Season well with salt and pepper.

While the ratatouille is simmering, prepare the aubergines. Turn on the grill (broiler) to a high heat and grease a large roasting tray (sheet pan) with 1 tablespoon oil. Lay half of the aubergine slices on the tray in a single layer and brush the tops with another 1 tablespoon oil. Grill the aubergines for 5 minutes or until golden. Transfer to a plate. Repeat with the second batch of aubergine slices. Set aide.

Cover the base of a 25 x 20-cm (10 x 8-inch) ovenproof dish with a layer of aubergine slices. Top with half of the ratatouille and then scatter over half of the grated vegan cheese.

Continued overleaf

2 aubergines (eggplants), sliced lengthways into 1-cm (⅓-inch) thick slices

75g (2½oz) vegan Italian hard cheese, grated (shredded)

Salt and freshly ground black pepper

To serve

Vegan garlic bread

Crisp green salad

Repeat these layers once more. Finish with a third layer of aubergine slices. You could scatter over a little more vegan cheese, if you prefer.

Bake in the hot oven for 20 minutes or until the top is golden and the lasagne is bubbling.

Remove the dish from the oven and allow the lasagne to cool for a few minutes before scattering over the reserved basil leaves. Serve with garlic bread and a crisp green salad.

COOK'S TIP This recipe is so versatile. You can either use cans of mixed beans, as I do, or choose your favourite type. Just make sure that the beans are in water or a tomato sauce and not a vinaigrette. You can use also dried herbs instead of fresh, if that's what you have in the cupboard.

VEGAN RED LENTIL, SPINACH AND DAHL LASAGNE

This recipe provides a quirky twist on the dahl that we all know and love. The use of coconut milk gives it an extra creamy taste, while the addition of an unexpected yet essential store cupboard ingredient may turn some heads! If you can handle the heat, add a few fresh chillies or dried chilli flakes to give the dish an extra punch, or just enjoy it with the warmth from the mellow spices.

Serves 3–4

2 tablespoons vegetable oil

1 onion, finely chopped

3 garlic cloves, diced

1½ teaspoons ground cumin

1 teaspoon ground turmeric

1 teaspoon paprika

1½ teaspoons curry powder (strength of your choosing)

250g (9oz) red lentils, rinsed

1½ tablespoons tomato paste (concentrated purée)

1½ tablespoons tomato ketchup

1 x 400-g (14-oz) can coconut milk

600ml (20¼fl oz) vegetable stock

300g (10½oz) fresh spinach

4 or 5 large garlic and herb naan breads

Salt and freshly ground black pepper

3 tablespoons mango chutney, to serve

Place a large frying pan (skillet) over a medium heat and add the oil. Once hot, add the onion and garlic and cook for 2 minutes before stirring in the cumin, turmeric, paprika and curry powder. Cook for a further 1 minute. Stir in the lentils followed by the tomato paste and tomato ketchup until combined. Next, pour in the coconut milk and leave to simmer for 25–30 minutes, slowly adding a ladleful of vegetable stock every few minutes to prevent the dahl from drying out.

When the lentils are tender, season well with salt and pepper.

Preheat the oven to 200°C/180°C fan/390°F/gas 6.

Sprinkle cold water over the base of a 25 x 20-cm (10 x 8-inch) ovenproof dish. Cover the base of the dish with a naan bread. Trim the naan bread to fit your dish and fill in any gaps. Spoon over half of the dahl mixture and top with half of the spinach leaves. Repeat these layers once more. Finish with the third layer of naan bread. Sprinkle a little more cold water across the top of the naan.

Bake in the hot oven for 15–20 minutes or until the naan is crispy and cooked. Keep an eye on the top of the lasagne to make sure that it does not burn. Remove the dish from the oven and allow the lasagne to cool for a few minutes before serving with a good dollop of mango chutney.

COOK'S TIP Instead of making your own dahl, you could always save time by buying a couple of pouches or pots of ready-made dahl to make this meal even quicker to throw together.

FOUR MUSHROOM AND FIVE CHEESE LASAGNE

As you might have guessed, I love lasagne. Although I shouldn't have a favourite, I have to confess that this one is an absolute cracker. Using such a variety of mushrooms gives a wide range of textures and flavours while the five – yes, five – cheeses in this recipe make the dish so gooey. It oozes deliciousness, so each bite really does melt in the mouth.

Serves 6

30g (1oz) dried porcini mushrooms

250ml (9fl oz) boiling water

4 tablespoons vegetable oil

1 leek, halved and finely sliced

10g (⅓oz) sage leaves, roughly chopped

150g (5½oz) Portobello mushrooms, roughly chopped

150g (5½oz) shiitake mushrooms, roughly chopped

300g (10½oz) chestnut mushrooms, roughly chopped

300g (10½oz) cream cheese

200ml (7fl oz) double (heavy) cream

100g (3½oz) vegetarian Saint Agur blue cheese, cut into chunks

1 teaspoon cornflour (cornstarch), made into a paste with a splash of water

Salt and freshly ground black pepper

Place the dried porcini mushrooms in a large bowl and cover with the boiling water. Leave to soak for 30 minutes. Once the mushrooms are rehydrated, remove them from the soaking liquid. Coarsely chop the mushrooms and set aside along with the soaking liquid.

Preheat the oven to 200°C/180°C fan/390°F/gas 6.

Heat 2 tablespoons oil in a large frying pan (skillet) over a medium heat. Add the leek with a pinch of salt and cook, stirring occasionally, for 10 minutes or until soft. Stir in the sage, then transfer the leeks and sage to a large bowl and set aside.

Add 1 tablespoon oil to the pan and add the Portobello and shiitake mushrooms. Cook over a high heat, stirring occasionally, for 2 minutes or until golden on all sides. Transfer the mushrooms to the bowl with the leeks.

Add another 1 tablespoon oil to the pan, add the chestnut mushrooms and cook for a further 2–3 minutes or until golden.

Return the leeks and mushroom mixture to the pan and cook everything for a further 2 minutes. Now, add the rehydrated porcini mushrooms and then gradually pour in the soaking liquid. Increase the heat to medium and simmer for 10 minutes or until the liquid has reduced. Season well with salt and pepper. Remove the pan from the heat and set aside.

In a separate bowl, mix together the cream cheese and cream to form a smooth sauce. Gradually add this sauce to the pan with the

Continued overleaf

To assemble

9–12 dried lasagne sheets

150g (5½oz) vegetarian mozzarella cheese

100g (3½oz) plant-based Camembert-style cheese, sliced

50g (1¾oz) vegan smoked applewood cheese, grated (shredded)

To serve

Crisp green salad

mushroom mixture. Place the pan back over a low heat, crumble in the blue cheese pieces and gently simmer for 10 minutes or until the sauce has thickened. You may need to add a little or all of the cornflour paste, if the sauce is still a little runny.

Cover the base of a 25 x 20-cm (10 x 8-inch) ovenproof dish with a layer of lasagne sheets. Trim the sheets to fit the dish, if necessary. Spoon one-third of the creamy mushroom mixture over the pasta, then tear over half of the mozzarella. Repeat these layers twice more. Finish with a fourth layer of lasagne sheets and then top with the reserved creamy sauce and the Camembert-style cheese and applewood smoked cheese.

Place the ovenproof dish on a baking tray and cover the dish with a piece of lightly oiled foil. Bake in the hot oven for 35–40 minutes or until bubbling and golden.

Remove the dish from the oven and allow the lasagne to rest for 10 minutes before slicing and serving with a crisp green salad.

COOK'S TIP Feel free to swap around the cheeses used in this recipe. Whatever you use, I do recommend adding one blue cheese to the sauce mix, a few soft cheeses that melt easily in the layers and then a good-quality hard cheese to grate over the top.

VEGAN TOFU, PUY LENTIL AND SPINACH LASAGNE

This simple but spicy lasagne is great to make for an easy midweek meal. It's packed with flavour and texture from the heat of the harissa and the crunch of the hazelnuts. I've found that marinating the tofu in advance really elevates the taste. Any leftovers work well for lunch the next day too – that's if you're able to resist the temptation to devour it all in one sitting; it really is moreish.

Serves 4

250g (9oz) firm tofu, dried and chopped into bite-size chunks

1 x 90-g (3-oz) jar harissa paste

2 tablespoons olive oil

2 x 400-g (14-oz) cans chopped tomatoes

1 x 250-g (9-oz) pouch ready-cooked Puy lentils

200g (7oz) fresh spinach

3–6 fresh lasagne sheets

50g (1¾oz) vegan Italian hard cheese, grated (shredded)

Salt and freshly ground black pepper

Place the tofu in a dish with 2 tablespoons harissa pasta and leave to marinate for 30 minutes or longer, if you have the time.

Preheat the oven to 200°C/180°C fan/390°F/gas 6.

Heat the oil in a large frying pan (skillet) over a medium heat. Add the marinated tofu and cook for 5 minutes or until brown and crispy. Next, stir in the chopped tomatoes and Puy lentils. Add 2 tablespoons harissa paste and season with salt and pepper to taste.

Reduce the heat to low and leave to simmer for around 20 minutes or until the sauce has thickened. Finally, stir in the spinach until wilted and then remove the pan from the heat.

Cover the base of a 25 x 20-cm (10 x 8-inch) ovenproof dish with a layer of lasagne sheets. Trim the sheets to fit the dish, if necessary. Spoon half the tofu and lentil mixture over the pasta.

Repeat these layers once more. Finish with a third layer of lasagne sheets. Spread the remaining harissa paste over the pasta and then scatter the cheese over the top.

Bake in the hot oven for 20 minutes or until the lasagne is bubbling and golden. Remove the dish from the oven and allow the lasagne to cool for 5 minutes before slicing and serving.

COOK'S TIP If you're cooking the lentils from scratch, either Puy or red lentils work well. Do allow for a longer cooking time and add plenty of stock to the pan to ensure the lentils cook thoroughly.

BLACK BEAN, COURGETTE AND QUINOA LASAGNE

You might not believe it at first, but this recipe really hits the spot. Using quinoa instead of minced (ground) beef is a total game changer, while the courgette sheets provide the perfect amount of bite. I've included the option to use sriracha hot sauce, but be warned this adds some fire to the lasagne – if you can handle the heat, go for it.

Serves 4

2 tablespoons vegetable oil

1 small onion, finely chopped

2 teaspoons dried oregano

1 x 400-g (14-oz) can black beans in water, drained

500g (1lb 2oz) tomato passata (strained tomatoes)

1 teaspoon caster (superfine) sugar

1 vegetable stock cube

1 x 200-g (7-oz) can sweetcorn kernels, drained

1 x 250-g (9-oz) pouch ready-cooked quinoa

250g (9oz) crème fraîche

2 tablespoons milk

2 tablespoons sriracha hot sauce (optional)

3 courgettes (zucchini), thinly sliced lengthways

50g (1¾oz) vegetarian or vegan Italian hard cheese, grated (shredded)

Salt and freshly ground black pepper

Preheat the oven to 200°C/180°C fan/390°F/gas 6.

Warm the oil in a frying pan (skillet) over a medium heat. Add the onion and oregano and cook for 3 minutes or until softened. Stir in the black beans, tomato passata and sugar. Crumble in the stock cube. Season well with salt and pepper. Reduce the heat to low and simmer for 10–15 minutes or until the sauce has thickened.

Next, add the sweetcorn and quinoa to the frying pan and stir to combine well. Leave to simmer for a further 5 minutes or until the sauce is silky and glossy.

Combine the crème fraîche and milk in a bowl. If using, stir in the sriracha hot sauce. Set aside for later.

Cover the base of a 25 x 20-cm (10 x 8-inch) ovenproof dish with a layer of courgette slices. Spoon half the quinoa and black bean mixture over the courgettes, then top with one-third of the crème fraîche. Repeat these layers once more. Finish with a third layer of courgette slices. Cover the courgettes with the remaining crème fraîche and then sprinkle over the grated hard cheese.

Bake in the hot oven for 25–30 minutes or until the lasagne is bubbling and golden. Remove the dish from the oven and allow the lasagne to cool for 5 minutes before slicing and serving.

COOK'S TIP You can use uncooked dried quinoa instead of a pouch of precooked quinoa. Before adding it to the tomato and black bean sauce, cook the dried quinoa in a separate pan with vegetable stock, which takes about 10 minutes.

VEGAN TOFU AND SWEET POTATO MASSAMAN LASAGNE

Like many, I used to be a little apprehensive of cooking tofu, but (after many mishaps) I've discovered it's such a versatile ingredient that takes on board the flavour of the marinades or sauces you're using, allowing it to be used in a whole array of dishes as an alternative to meat. The earthy sweet potatoes work wonderfully with the Massaman sauce in this lasagne.

Serves 4–6

6 tablespoons olive oil, plus extra for brushing

3 aubergines (eggplants), cut into 3-mm (⅛-inch) thick slices

25g (¾oz) cornflour (cornstarch)

250g (9oz) firm tofu, dried and chopped into 2-cm (¾-inch) cubes

2 sweet potatoes, peeled and chopped into 2-cm (¾-inch) cubes

1 x 190-g (6¾-oz) jar vegan Massaman curry paste or 'free-from' mild curry paste

2 x 400-ml (14fl-oz) cans coconut milk

50g (1¾oz) unsweetened desiccated coconut

Salt and freshly ground black pepper

Warm a frying pan (skillet) over a high heat. Drizzle 4 tablespoons oil over the aubergine slices and fry in batches for 5 minutes on each side or until softened and golden. Set aside on kitchen paper.

Preheat the oven to 200°C/180°C fan/390°F/gas 6.

Put the cornflour in a bowl and season to taste. Add in the tofu cubes and toss until fully coated.

Drizzle 2 tablespoons oil into the same pan over a medium heat and toast the tofu until golden on all sides. Remove from the pan and set aside for later.

Using the same pan, cook the sweet potato over a medium heat for 2 minutes. Stir in the curry paste and add the coconut milk. Reduce the heat to low and simmer for 25–30 minutes or until the sweet potato is tender and the sauce has thickened. If the sauce is too runny, add 1 teaspoon cornflour paste to thicken the sauce before assembling the lasagne.

Brush the base and sides of a 25 x 20-cm (10 x 8-inch) ovenproof dish with oil and cover with one-third of the aubergine slices. Spoon over half the tofu and sweet potato curry. Repeat these layers once more. Finish with a third layer of aubergine slices, brushed with a little more oil.

Bake in the hot oven for 35 minutes, then sprinkle the desiccated coconut over the top of the lasagne and return to the oven for a further 5 minutes. Remove the dish from the oven and allow the lasagne to cool for 5 minutes before serving.

VEGAN PULLED JACKFRUIT, SWEET POTATO AND RED CABBAGE LASAGNE

This dish is a vegan dream, providing a near identical but veggie alternative to a barbecue classic. I suspect the most ardent of meat eaters could be swayed by this lasagne, with both the texture and appearance of jackfruit being easily mistaken for pork. What's more, pulled jackfruit takes under 30 minutes to make in comparison to the hours spent slowly tenderising a meat joint.

Serves 6

2 tablespoons vegetable oil

1 red onion, finely sliced

1 teaspoon ground cumin

2 teaspoons paprika

2 teaspoons chilli powder

1 x 400-g (14-oz) can chopped tomatoes

140ml (5fl oz) barbecue sauce

1 x 400-g (14-oz) can jackfruit, drained

¼ red cabbage (approx. 200g/7oz), finely sliced

3 medium sweet potatoes, peeled and sliced into 3-mm (¹⁄₁₆-inch) thick discs

50g (1¾oz) vegan Italian hard cheese, grated (shredded)

Salt and freshly ground black pepper

To serve

Sliced spring onions (scallions)

Chopped parsley

Coconut yogurt

Heat the oil in a large frying pan (skillet) over a medium heat. Add the onion with a pinch of salt and cook for 2 minutes or until soft. Next, add the spices, chopped tomatoes, 100ml (3½fl oz) barbecue sauce and 50ml (1¾fl oz) water. Stir to combine before adding the jackfruit and red cabbage. Reduce the heat to low and leave to simmer for 20 minutes, stirring occasionally, until the sauce has thickened and the jackfruit has shredded. Season with salt and pepper to taste.

Preheat the oven to 200°C/180°C fan/390°F/gas 6.

Cover the base of a 25 x 20-cm (10 x 8-inch) ovenproof dish with a layer of sweet potato slices, then top with half of the pulled jackfruit. Repeat these layers once more. Finish with a third layer of sweet potato slices. Top with the remaining barbecue sauce and scatter over the vegan cheese.

Place the dish in the hot oven and bake the lasagne for 50 minutes or until the sweet potato has softened and the top is golden.

Remove the dish from the oven and allow the lasagne to cool for 10 minutes. Scatter over the spring onions and parsley before serving with spoonfuls of coconut yogurt on the side.

COOK'S TIP Ideally, use a mandoline to slice the sweet potatoes for slices of a consistent thickness. The cooking time might vary depending on how thick the slices are. You're aiming for a sharp knife to easily glide through all the potato layers when it's cooked.

FALAFEL, HALLOUMI AND RED CABBAGE STACK

Simple and speedy to prepare ahead of time, this no-bake layered dish is a great one to enjoy at a gathering with friends or family. It's packed with contrasting tastes and textures, with the earthy falafel, salty halloumi and sharp cabbage providing great flavours, while the pomegranate seeds add a burst of sweetness and extra crunch.

Serves 6

6 pita breads

200g (7oz) falafel balls

1 tablespoon vegetable oil

2 x 250-g (9-oz) blocks vegetarian halloumi, each sliced into 6 lengthways

1 x 200-g (7-oz) tub hummus

1 x 60-g (2-oz) bag rocket (arugula)

1 x 440-g (15½-oz) jar pickled red cabbage, drained

100g (3½oz) sundried tomatoes, roughly chopped

75g (2½oz) pomegranate seeds

2 tablespoons tahini

Lightly toast the pita breads, then separate each one into two large rounds.

Warm a large frying pan (skillet) over a medium heat. Add the falafel and cook for 3 minutes, turning frequently so they turn golden and crispy on all sides. Transfer to a plate and set aside.

Warm the oil in the frying pan. Add the halloumi and fry on both sides until golden and crispy. Transfer to a plate and leave to cool.

Cover the base of a 25 x 20-cm (10 x 8-inch) with a layer of 4 pita halves. Spread 3 tablespoons hummus over the pita, then top with half of the grilled halloumi slices. Scatter half of the rocket leaves over the halloumi, then add 3 heaped tablespoons pickled red cabbage and half of the chopped sundried tomatoes. Crumble over half of the falafel in a layer, then scatter over one-third of the pomegranate seeds.

Repeat these layers once more. Finish with a third layer of pita halves, then drizzle over the tahini and top with any remaining pomegranate seeds and rocket leaves.

Cover the dish and then chill in the fridge until ready to serve.

COOK'S TIP Substitute the classic plain hummus for any flavoured version you prefer. This recipe works just as well with sweet red pepper hummus or spicy chilli hummus.

SWEET

AMARETTI AND NECTARINE LASAGNE

Almonds, glorious almonds! The nutty flavour of almonds runs throughout this dessert, from the crunchy amaretti biscuits to the boozy amaretto liqueur, making this a ravishingly indulgent dish. It's the perfect dinner-party dessert as it can be prepared well in advance, minimising the time spent in the kitchen once your guests have arrived. Why not serve this with a wee tipple of amaretto liqueur, too?

Serves 4

6 nectarines, pitted and sliced into wedges

3 tablespoons apricot jam (preserve)

125ml (4½fl oz) amaretto liqueur (or orange juice for an alcohol-free version)

100g (3½oz) raspberries (fresh or frozen)

70g (2½oz) salted butter

4 tablespoons runny honey

250g (9oz) amaretti biscuits, crushed

50g (1¾oz) flaked (slivered) almonds

Crème fraîche or ice cream, to serve

Preheat the oven to 200°C/180°C fan/390°F/gas 6.

Place the nectarines, apricot jam and amaretto in a large bowl and gently stir together until well mixed. Carefully fold through the raspberries and set aside.

Place the butter and honey in a saucepan over a low heat and leave until the butter has melted. Remove the pan from the heat and tip in the crushed amaretti biscuits. Stir to combine until the biscuits are fully coated in the melted butter. Set aside for later.

Cover the base of a 15-cm (6-inch) round ovenproof dish with one-third of the honeyed amaretti biscuits, pressing them down to compact the layer. Top with half of the fruity mixture.

Repeat these layers once more. Finish with a third layer of the crushed amaretti biscuits and scatter over the flaked almonds.

Bake in the hot oven for 25–30 minutes, or until the lasagne is bubbling, the top biscuit layer is crisp and the almonds are golden.

Remove the dish from the oven and allow the lasagne to cool slightly before serving with crème fraîche or ice cream.

COOK'S TIP When nectarines are not in season, you can make this dessert using canned peaches instead.

ESPRESSO MARTINI TRIFLE

An espresso martini is one of the most instantly recognisable cocktails, so I wanted to create a sweet trifle that gives a nod to this popular drink. This dish has a real wow factor and is a spectacular end to any dinner party. If you prefer, you can swap the classic chocolate-coated coffee beans for chocolate-dipped strawberries to bring a little goodness to this delightfully naughty dessert.

Serves 6

3 tablespoons double (heavy) cream

1½ tablespoons instant coffee granules

250g (9oz) mascarpone cheese

30g (1oz) icing (confectioners') sugar, sifted

1 x 400-g (14-oz) carton fresh vanilla custard

50g (1¾oz) dark (bittersweet) chocolate (at least 40% cocoa solids)

6 triple chocolate chip muffins, thinly sliced

4 tablespoons coffee rum liqueur (or a shot of espresso for an alcohol-free version)

To decorate

300ml (10½fl oz) double (heavy) cream, lightly whipped

Handful of chocolate-covered coffee beans

Pour the cream into a heatproof bowl and warm for 20 seconds in a microwave. Stir the coffee granules into the warm cream until dissolved. Set aside to cool.

Put the mascarpone in a mixing bowl and add the icing sugar. Pour in the coffee cream and stir to combine fully.

Put the vanilla custard and dark chocolate in a saucepan and warm over a low heat. Stir continuously until the chocolate is melted. Remove the pan from the heat and set aside to cool.

Cover the base of a 25 x 20-cm (10 x 8-inch) serving dish with a layer of muffin slices. Drizzle over half of the coffee rum liqueur and allow to soak into the muffins. Next, spread over half of the coffee mascarpone and top with half of the chocolate custard. Alternatively, layer the trifle in individual martini glasses. Repeat these layers once more. Place in the fridge for at least 1 hour.

When ready to serve, whisk the cream to soft peaks. Top the serving dish or glasses with the whipped cream and decorate with a few chocolate-covered coffee beans.

COOK'S TIP Rather than coffee beans, you could decorate with chocolate-dipped strawberries instead. Melt 50g (1¾oz) white chocolate in a heatproof bowl set over a pan of boiling water or in a microwave. Lay a large sheet of parchment paper over a tray. Clean 225g (8oz) strawberries, then, holding them by their stalk or leaves, dip the bottom half of each berry into the melted chocolate to coat and then place on the parchment paper. Put the chocolate-dipped strawberries in the fridge for 30 minutes to set.

RHUBARB, ELDERFLOWER AND CUSTARD CRÊPES

Full of quintessential summer flavours that, for me, evoke childhood memories of an old-fashioned sweetie shop, this dessert is bursting with a tasty nostalgia. Rhubarb is in season in the UK from April to July and so this dish makes a perfect summertime dessert but can be enjoyed at other times by using either frozen or canned fruit. The addition of elderflower adds a refreshing and fragrant touch.

Serves 4

100ml (3½fl oz) elderflower cordial

75g (2½oz) caster (superfine) sugar

10g (⅓oz) cornflour (cornstarch)

650g (1lb 7oz) rhubarb stalks, chopped into 2.5-cm (1-inch) pieces

4–6 crêpes (available from major supermarkets)

500ml (17fl oz) ready-made vanilla custard

15g (½oz) icing (confectioners') sugar

Place the elderflower cordial, sugar and cornflour in a saucepan over a low heat. Stir continuously until the sugar is dissolved. Add the chopped rhubarb and simmer on a low heat, stirring continuously for 15 minutes or until the rhubarb has broken down and the mixture thickens to a jam-like consistency. Remove the pan from the heat and set aside to cool.

Preheat the oven to 180°C/160°C fan/350°F/gas 4.

Cover the base of a 25 x 20-cm (10 x 8-inch) ovenproof dish with a layer of the crêpes. Trim them to fit the shape of the dish, if necessary. Spoon half of the rhubarb and elderflower compote over the crêpes, then top with half of the custard.

Repeat these layers of crêpes, fruit compote and custard once more. Finish with a third layer of crêpes.

Cover the dish with foil and place in the hot oven for 20 minutes or until the custard is bubbling.

Remove the dish from the oven and allow to rest for 5 minutes. Dust with icing sugar before serving. This dessert can be enjoyed either hot or cold.

COOK'S TIP Using ready-made custard and crêpes saves plenty of time when you're making this dessert, but feel free to make your own from scratch if you prefer.

NEAPOLITAN POTS

Usually served as three distinct flavours of ice cream, I've turned this instantly recognisable dessert into layers of chocolate mousse, fresh mango and pineapple, topped with strawberry cheesecake, retaining the traditional trio of colours. Switch up the flavours by exchanging strawberry jam (preserve) for raspberry or using canned peaches when mango and pineapple are not in season.

Serves 4

200g (7oz) milk or dark (bittersweet) chocolate, broken into chunks

400ml (14fl oz) double (heavy) cream

400g (14oz) cream cheese

4 tablespoons icing (confectioners') sugar, plus extra for dusting

6 heaped tablespoons strawberry jam (preserve)

1 large mango, peeled, pitted and thinly sliced

1 medium pineapple, peeled, cored and thinly sliced

8 strawberries, hulled and sliced

Place the chocolate in a heatproof bowl and melt over a pan of simmering water. Do not let the bowl touch the bubbling water. Set aside to cool.

In a large bowl, whip the cream by hand or with an electric beater until stiff peaks form. Fold the cooled chocolate into the whipped cream until fully combined.

In a separate bowl, combine the cream cheese, icing sugar and jam to make a strawberry cheesecake mixture.

Assemble the dessert in four large wine glasses. Place 2 heaped tablespoons of the chocolate mousse in the bottom of each wine glass and level the surface. Top with thin slices of fresh mango and pineapple. Finish with 2 heaped tablespoons of the strawberry cheesecake mixture. Repeat these layers once more.

Place the glasses in the fridge for 30 minutes to set the dessert. Immediately before serving, top each dessert with some sliced strawberries and then dust with a little icing sugar.

COOK'S TIP If your wine glasses have quite a narrow opening and a spoon does not fit, fill a piping (pastry) bag with the chocolate mousse and pipe it into each glass. Do the same with the strawberry cheesecake mixture to create neat layers.

BLUEBERRY 'BREAD AND BUTTER' PUDDING WITH LEMON CURD

This scrumptious layered bake is so speedy yet so simple to make. This recipe is perfect for using up those leftover muffins lurking in the cake tin. With a few nifty shortcuts using frozen berries and ready-made custard, you can rustle up this dish in a matter of minutes, I promise.

Serves 6

150g (5½oz) blueberries (fresh or frozen)

Zest and juice of 1 lemon

8 blueberry muffins, cut into 2-cm (¾-inch) thick slices

6 tablespoons lemon curd

75g (2½oz) dark (bittersweet) chocolate chips

500ml (17fl oz) ready-made vanilla custard

100ml (3½fl oz) double (heavy) cream

2 tablespoons demerara sugar

Combine the blueberries with the lemon zest and juice in a bowl. Mix well and set aside.

Cover the base of a 25 x 20-cm (10 x 8-inch) ovenproof dish with one-third of the muffin slices. Carefully spread half of the lemon curd over the muffins and then scatter over half of the blueberries and half of the chocolate chips. Repeat these layers once more. Finish with a third layer of muffin slices.

Combine the custard and cream in a bowl, then pour this mixture over the top layer of muffin slices. Press the muffin layer down to make sure each slice is submerged in the custard mixture and leave to soak for 15 minutes.

Meanwhile, preheat the oven to 200°C/180°C fan/390°F/gas 6.

Place the ovenproof dish on a baking tray and bake in the hot oven for 25–30 minutes or until the custard is bubbling. Sprinkle the demerara sugar over the top of the custard and return to the oven for a further 5 minutes or until golden.

Remove the dish from the oven and set aside to cool for a few minutes before serving.

COOK'S TIP You can use either store-bought or homemade muffins in this recipe. As odd as this may sound, the staler the muffins are, the better, as they soak up even more of the curd and custard. You can change up the flavours in a number of ways. Exchange the blueberry muffins for another sponge cake or cupcake, the lemon curd for your favourite jam (preserve), and the chocolate chips for fudge pieces or even chopped nuts.

APRICOT, PISTACHIO AND CHOCOLATE GANACHE TRAYBAKE

This sweet traybake takes 15 minutes to rustle up, so it can be made whenever a last-minute dessert is needed. The sticky apricots and roasted pistachios are a winning combination, while the hint of aromatic cardamom complements the intensely indulgent chocolate ganache. This prepare-ahead traybake is perfect to round off a dinner party, but is also a tasty treat to be enjoyed with a cup of tea.

Serves 8

250g (9oz) shelled unsalted pistachios

500g (1lb 2oz) dried apricots

2 teaspoons vanilla extract

4 tablespoons runny honey

150g (5½oz) dark (bittersweet) chocolate, broken into very small pieces

300ml (10½fl oz) double (heavy) cream

10 cardamom pods

Icing (confectioners') sugar, for dusting

Preheat the oven to 200°C/180°C fan/390°F/gas 6.

Spread the pistachios over a baking sheet and toast in the hot oven for 5 minutes or until golden and fragrant. Remove from the oven and set aside to cool.

Place the apricots in a food processor and pulse until finely chopped. Add the cooled pistachios, vanilla extract and honey and pulse again until the mixture forms a sticky 'dough'.

Place the chocolate in a heatproof bowl. Combine the cream and cardamom pods in a saucepan and bring to a gentle simmer, but do not let it boil. Remove the cardamom pods and immediately pour the hot cream over the chocolate. Slowly stir with a metal spoon to combine until the chocolate is fully melted. Set aside.

Line a 20 x 20-cm (8 x 8-inch) dish with parchment paper. Press one-third of the apricot mixture into the base of the prepared dish. Top with half of the chocolate ganache, spreading it to completely cover the apricot layer. Repeat these layers once more. Finish with a third layer of the apricot mixture.

Place in the fridge and chill the traybake for at least 3 hours or until the layers have set. When ready to serve, dust with icing sugar before slicing.

COOK'S TIP Instead of using the cardamom pods, you can use 2 teaspoons ground cardamom instead. Or you can add a different flavour to the chocolate ganache, such as orange zest.

SALTED CARAMEL AND RICE PUDDING LASAGNE

Rice pudding is such a nostalgic dish, it brings back childhood memories for many. However, in this recipe, I take that rather traditional milk pudding and bring it right into the twenty-first century as a lasagne! When the hot and creamy vanilla rice meets the layers of nutty, salted caramel shards, you will be hit by an irresistibly addictive taste that will have you hooked on this sweet treat forever more.

Serves 4

140g (5oz) granulated (white) sugar

40g (1½oz) blanched (skinned) hazelnuts, halved

2 teaspoons coarse sea salt flakes

600g (1lb 5oz) ready-made rice pudding

1 teaspoon vanilla bean paste

25ml (¾fl oz) double (heavy) cream

2 tablespoons salted caramel sauce

Lay a large sheet of parchment paper on a chopping board, ready for the caramel.

Place a heavy-based saucepan over a low heat. Pour the sugar into the pan and add 4 tablespoons water. As the sugar dissolves, turn up the heat to medium and leave until the sugar turns to a golden caramel. Resist every temptation to stir the pan – if you do, the sugar will crystallise. Add the chopped hazelnuts to the caramel and then immediately pour it onto the parchment paper in a thin, even layer, using a spatula to scrape the pan. Sprinkle the salt flakes over the caramel and leave to cool for 10 minutes. Using a sharp knife, chop the caramel into 12–16 shards.

Meanwhile, place a large saucepan over a low heat and add the rice pudding along with the vanilla paste and cream. Stir to combine and leave to simmer for 5 minutes or until bubbling.

When ready to eat, place around 50g (1¾oz) of the rice pudding in each of four ramekins. Lay a caramel shard on top of the rice pudding in each ramekin.

Repeat these layers of rice pudding and caramel shards twice more. Finish with a third layer of nutty caramel. Drizzle over the salted caramel sauce before serving.

COOK'S TIP Make the caramel shards in advance but only assemble this dish just as you're about to eat it. The hot rice pudding melts the cold caramel shards, giving you a crunchy yet gooey dessert!

CHERRY AND HAZELNUT MERINGUE LAYER CAKE

This easy-bake, layered meringue cake is one for the whole family to enjoy. The creamy, chocolatey mascarpone and juicy, sweet cherries layered between crunchy, nutty meringue make for the perfect dessert. A little goes a long way with this tasty sweet treat. This meringue is best enjoyed when just made, but I doubt there will be much left after friends and loved ones have all devoured a slice.

Serves 8–10

For the meringue

150g (5½oz) blanched (skinned) whole hazelnuts

200g (7oz) golden caster (superfine) sugar

100g (3½oz) light muscovado (light brown) sugar

6 large egg whites (about 190g in weight)

1½ teaspoons white wine vinegar

1½ teaspoons cornflour (cornstarch)

For the chocolate mascarpone

375g (14oz) mascarpone cheese

90g (3oz) icing (confectioners') sugar, plus extra to dust

35g (1½oz) unsweetened cocoa powder

200ml (7fl oz) double (heavy) cream

Preheat the oven to 200°C/180°C fan/390°F/gas 6.

Place the hazelnuts on a baking sheet and toast in the oven for 8–10 minutes or until golden and nutty. Remove from the oven and set aside to cool. Once cool, place the hazelnuts in a food processor or blender with 100g (3½oz) golden caster sugar and blitz until they look like breadcrumbs. Be careful not to overprocess the hazelnuts to a paste.

Reduce the oven temperature to 140°C/120°C fan/280°F/gas 1.

Cut three sheets of parchment paper to the size of a 20-cm (8-inch) baking sheet. Alternatively, mark out a 20-cm (8-inch) square with a ruler and pencil on one side of each sheet. Turn the paper over and use to line three large baking sheets.

Combine the light muscovado sugar and the remaining golden caster sugar in a mixing bowl and set aside.

In a spotlessly clean, grease-free, large mixing bowl, whisk the egg whites until they form soft peaks. (Any traces of grease in the bowl will prevent the egg whites whisking to their full volume.) Gradually spoon in the sugars, whisking continuously until stiff and shiny peaks form. Finally, whisk in the vinegar and cornflour to the meringue mixture. Using a spatula, lightly fold in the toasted hazelnut and sugar mixture.

Divide the meringue mixture evenly between the three baking sheets, spreading it within the marked squares. Using a palette knife warmed in boiling water, smooth the top of two of the

Continued overleaf

To assemble

100g (3½oz) blanched (skinned) hazelnuts, halved

300g (10½oz) fresh cherries

25g (¾oz) milk chocolate

meringues so they are as flat and even as possible. The third meringue doesn't need to be smooth as it will top the cake.

Place the baking sheets in the oven for 1 hour 15 minutes or until the meringue is cooked. Switch off the oven, open the door slightly and leave the meringues inside to cool completely. To check the meringues are cooked, peel the parchment paper away from the base – it should pull back easily without sticking.

Meanwhile, in a separate bowl, mix together the mascarpone, icing sugar and cocoa powder. Whisk the cream until it just holds its shape, then whisk the cream into the mascarpone mixture.

Set aside one-third of the cherries, preferably with their stalks still attached. Halve or quarter the remaining cherries and remove the stones (pits).

To assemble, place one of the flat-top meringues on a serving platter or cake stand then spread over one-third of the chocolate mascarpone mixture. Top with half of the pitted cherries and one-third of the halved hazelnuts. Repeat these layers once more.

Finish with a third layer of meringue, using the one that you didn't flatten the surface of, then top that with the remaining chocolate mascarpone. Halve a few of the reserved cherries and decorate the top of the meringue cake with the whole and halved fresh cherries and remaining halved hazelnuts. Grate (shred) the milk chocolate over the top of the cake to decorate.

Alternatively, place the milk chocolate in a small heatproof bowl and melt either set over a saucepan of boiling water or carefully in the microwave. Once fully melted, set aside to cool before drizzling over the top of the meringue. Allow the chocolate to set before slicing and serving.

COOK'S TIP I've used fresh cherries in this recipe, but you could use canned cherries, or other canned fruits such as pears or peaches, when fresh cherries are out of season. Drain the canned cherries from their syrup before layering the meringues as the liquid from the cherries can make the meringue slightly soggy.

BANANA AND SPECULOOS LASAGNE

This sweet lasagne is so naughty yet totally irresistible. Inspired by the classic banoffee pie, this dish is certainly a treat for anyone with a sweet tooth. What with the tempting caramel flavour from the speculoos spread and the creaminess of the condensed milk teasing you with every bite, this silky dessert will leave you wanting more.

Serves 4

12–16 white bread slices (depending on loaf size), crusts removed

6 tablespoons speculoos spread or other cookie butter

250g (9oz) mascarpone cheese

125g (4½oz) condensed milk

3 bananas, peeled and thinly sliced

3 large stroopwafel or other Dutch caramel waffle cookies, chopped into bite-size pieces

Preheat the oven to 200°C/180°C fan/390°F/gas 6.

Cover one side of each slice of white bread evenly with the speculoos spread.

Combine the mascarpone and condensed milk in a large bowl, whisking until smooth and creamy.

Cover the base of a 20 x 20-cm (8 x 8-inch) deep-sided ovenproof dish with one-third of the speculoos-covered bread. You may need to trim the slices to fit your dish. Lay one-third of the banana slices over the bread. Next, cover the banana with one-third of the sweet mascarpone.

Repeat the layers of bread, bananas and mascarpone twice more.

Cover the dish with foil and place in the oven for 15–20 minutes or until warmed through. Remove the foil, scatter over the stroopwafel pieces and return to the oven for a further 5 minutes or until the caramel is oozing out over the top of the lasagne.

Remove the dish from the oven and allow to rest for at least 15–20 minutes or until the caramel sauce has firmed up. Slice and serve, scooping up any of the extra sauce to drizzle over.

COOK'S TIP If you can't find stroopwafels or caramel waffle cookies, feel free to top this dessert with fudge chunks or even speculoos biscuit crumbs instead.

COOKIES AND CREAM LASAGNE

You're in for a treat with this lasagne. If, like me, you always struggle to choose just one pudding to have, this recipe allows you to enjoy two classic sweet treats in one. With gooey white chocolate chip and raspberry cookies layered between creamy vanilla cheesecake filling and with extra sweetness from fresh raspberries, I promise this lasagne will become your new go-to dessert.

Serves 4

For the cookies

80g (3oz) butter

130g (4½oz) dark muscovado (dark brown) sugar

1½ teaspoons vanilla extract

2 eggs

180g (6½oz) plain (all-purpose) flour

15g (½oz) cornflour (cornstarch)

½ teaspoon bicarbonate of soda (baking soda)

80g (3oz) frozen raspberries

80g (3oz) white chocolate chips

For the cheesecake filling

150ml (5½fl oz) double (heavy) cream

250g (9oz) cream cheese

1 teaspoon vanilla bean paste

50g (1¾oz) icing (confectioners') sugar, plus extra for dusting

To serve

200g (7oz) fresh raspberries

Preheat the oven to 200°C/180°C fan/390°F/gas 6.

To make the cookies, pulse together the butter and sugar in a food processor until light and fluffy. Add the vanilla extract and eggs, then pulse again. The mixture may look curdled, but that's fine.

Sift the flour into a large mixing bowl and add the cornflour and bicarbonate of soda. Pour in the wet ingredients and stir to combine. Fold in the frozen raspberries and white chocolate chips until everything is fully incorporated and the mixture forms a soft dough. If the dough appears a little dry, add a splash of milk. Be careful not to make the dough too wet, however, as the frozen raspberries will also add moisture to the dough.

Line a 28 x 18-cm (11 x 7-inch) baking sheet with parchment paper. Spread the dough over the lined sheet and bake in the hot oven for 15–20 minutes or until cooked through.

Remove from the oven and divide the cookie slab into three equal rectangles while warm. Allow the cookies to cool in the tray for 10 minutes before transferring to a wire rack to cool completely.

Meanwhile, make the cheesecake filling. Whisk the cream in a bowl either with a balloon whisk or an electric beater to form soft peaks. Fold the cream cheese and vanilla bean paste into the whipped cream. Finally, stir in the icing sugar.

To assemble, place one cookie slab on a serving platter. Cover with one-third of the cheesecake filling and finally top with one-third of the fresh raspberries. Repeat these layers twice more. Dust with icing sugar and serve straight away.

KEY LIME SHORTBREAD STACK

I fondly remember my mum's homemade version of custard creams; the biscuit tin was always full to the brim with that buttery delight. This is my take on that childhood staple, the custard cream, but also taking inspiration from another classic, key lime pie, with the addition of a zesty citrus filling.

Serves 8

For the lime cream

300g (10½oz) condensed milk

220ml (7½fl oz) double (heavy) cream

Zest and juice of 4 limes

For the shortbread

400g (14oz) salted butter

115g (4oz) icing (confectioners') sugar

400g (14oz) self-raising flour, plus an extra 2–3 tablespoons for dusting

115g (4oz) custard powder

2 teaspoons vanilla extract

Caster (superfine) sugar, for sprinkling

To assemble

4 tablespoons lime curd

To make the lime cream, whisk the condensed milk and cream to soft peaks. Lightly whisk in the lime zest and juice. Do not over-beat the cream as the juice makes it thicken quickly. Place in the fridge for 1 hour to set.

In a large mixing bowl, beat together the butter and icing sugar until smooth. Gradually sift in the flour and custard powder and stir until well combined. Add the vanilla extract, then lightly knead the dough to gather it into one firm ball.

Lightly flour a piece of parchment paper. Place the dough on the paper and roll out into a rectangle measuring 27 x 20 cm (10½ x 8 inches) and 1.5cm (½ inch) thick. Lightly score two lines across the dough, dividing it into three 20 x 9-cm (8 x 3½-inch) rectangles (this makes it easier to cut to size once baked). Prick the dough all over with a fork. Lift the parchment paper and transfer the dough to a baking sheet. Chill in the fridge for 20 minutes.

Preheat the oven to 200°C/180°C fan/390°F/gas 6.

Bake in the hot oven for 12–15 minutes or until golden brown.

Remove from the oven. Immediately divide the shortbread into three, cutting along the scored lines. Sprinkle with a little caster sugar. Allow to cool on the tray for 10 minutes, then transfer to a wire rack to cool completely.

To assemble immediately before serving, place one of the shortbread slabs on a serving dish or platter. Spread over half of the key lime cream and top with half the lime curd. Repeat these layers once more. Finish with the third shortbread slab. Serve straight away so that the shortbread remains crisp.

CHOCOLATE S'MORES BITES

This is a fantastic make-ahead sweet treat. All the components can be prepared a day in advance, so you only need to leave your guests briefly to assemble dessert. Even better, there's no squabbling over portion sizes with this pud as the recipe makes deliciously dinky, individual sweet lasagnes.

Serves 8

For the biscuit base

16 chocolate digestive biscuits (graham crackers)

60g (2oz) butter

For the marshmallow mascarpone

200g (7oz) mascarpone cheese

100g (3½oz) marshmallow fluff (available from major supermarkets)

For the chocolate mousse

90g (3oz) milk or dark (bittersweet) chocolate

15g (½oz) butter

90ml (3fl oz) double (heavy) cream

2 eggs, separated

25g (¾oz) caster (superfine) sugar

To serve

40g (1½oz) mini marshmallows

Preheat the oven to 200°C/180°C fan/390°F/gas 6 and place eight paper muffin cases in a nine- or twelve-hole muffin tray.

Place 8 of the biscuits in a blender and blitz to fine crumbs. Alternatively, crush them in a sturdy plastic bag with a rolling pin. Melt the butter in a saucepan over a low heat, then tip in the crushed biscuits and stir to combine. Divide the biscuit base mixture evenly between the muffin cases and press down with the back of a teaspoon to form a firm, smooth base. Bake in the hot oven for 8 minutes. Remove from the oven and set aside to cool. Once completely cool, lift the paper muffin cases out of the tray and then peel away the paper cases to leave the biscuit base.

Combine the mascarpone and marshmallow fluff in a bowl. Beat vigorously until smooth and creamy. Set aside in the fridge.

Melt the chocolate and butter in a saucepan over a low heat. Remove the pan from the heat and set aside to cool completely. In a separate bowl, whisk the cream until nearly stiff. Stir in the 2 egg yolks. Once the chocolate is cold, gradually stir it into the whipped cream until combined and the mixture has thickened.

In a third bowl, whisk the egg whites and sugar until soft peaks form. Gradually fold the egg whites into the chocolate cream with a metal spoon. Place in the fridge to set for at least 1 hour.

To assemble, place the individual biscuit bases on a serving platter. Gently spread a tablespoon of marshmallow mascarpone over each base. Place a whole chocolate digestive (chocolate side up) on top, then top with a tablespoon of the chocolate mousse. Finally scatter over a small handful of mini marshmallows on top. Chill for 30 minutes to allow the s'mores to set before serving.

MINCEMEAT, CRANBERRY AND ORANGE TRAYBAKE

I've taken some of my favourite festive flavours to create this buttery, fruity traybake; with the best bits of a Christmas cake and yuletide mince pies and finished off with a delightfully crumbly topping.

Serves 8–10

75g (2½oz) salted butter

320g (11¼oz) ready-rolled shortcrust pastry

1 x 400-g (14-oz) jar mincemeat

100g (3½oz) cranberry sauce

150g (5½oz) frozen cranberries, thawed and drained

Zest and juice of 2 large oranges

60g (2oz) plain (all-purpose) flour

60g (2oz) ground almonds (almond flour)

60g (2oz) golden caster (superfine) sugar

25g (¾oz) icing (confectioners') sugar

250g (9oz) marzipan

30g (1oz) flaked (slivered) almonds

Vanilla ice cream, to serve

Preheat the oven to 200°C/180°C fan/390°F/gas 6 and use a little of the butter to grease a 20-cm (8-inch) square cake tin.

Unroll the pastry sheet and use to line the greased tin, pressing it into the corners and up the sides. Trim any excess pastry with a sharp knife and prick the base with a fork. Place parchment paper in the tin and fill with baking beans or dried grains. Bake in the hot oven for 12–15 minutes or until the pastry is golden. Remove the baking beans and paper and return to the oven for 3 minutes to ensure the pastry case is baked. Leave to cool in the tin.

In a bowl, combine the mincemeat, cranberry sauce, cranberries and orange zest. Gradually pour in half of the orange juice. (Depending on the juiciness of the oranges, you may not need it all.) The mixture should not be too runny.

In a separate bowl, rub the remaining butter into the flour, ground almonds and caster sugar until it resembles fine breadcrumbs.

Dust a clean work surface and rolling pin with icing sugar. Roll out the marzipan to a square just slightly less than 20cm (8 inches).

To assemble the traybake, spoon half of the mincemeat mixture into the pastry case inside the tin. Top with the rolled-out marzipan. Cover the marzipan with the remaining mincemeat and then finish with the crumble mixture scattered over the top.

Place the tin on a baking tray and bake in the oven for 30 minutes. Remove from the oven, sprinkle the flaked almonds on top and return to the oven for a further 10 minutes or until the crumble is crispy and the almonds are golden. Set aside for 10 minutes before serving with a scoop or two of vanilla ice cream.

CELEBRATIONS

CHRISTMAS DINNER LASAGNE

This festive recipe was the very start of my adventures in lasagne making, and the inspiration behind this entire book. It's a dish that has been enjoyed by family, friends and even Jamie Oliver! It's packed with all the Christmas goodies we know and love, from chestnuts to chipolatas and Brussels sprouts to bread sauce. It has everything Christmas-related (and more) you could ever dream of and it allows you to serve up a Christmas dinner with all the trimmings in one dish.

Serves 4

200g (7oz) Brussels sprouts, halved

3 tablespoons vegetable oil

8 'pigs in blankets' (pork chipolatas wrapped in smoked streaky bacon)

1 onion, finely diced

3 carrots, peeled and finely diced

500g (1lb 2oz) minced (ground) turkey

2 tablespoons turkey or chicken gravy granules

200ml (7fl oz) boiling water

3 tablespoons cranberry sauce, plus extra to serve

800g (1lb 12oz) potatoes, peeled and sliced into 2-mm (1/16-inch) thick discs

170g (6oz) chestnut stuffing or your favourite stuffing mix

4 thyme sprigs, leaves only, or sage leaves

Preheat the oven to 200°C/180°C fan/390°F/gas 6.

Toss the Brussels sprouts in 1 teaspoon oil. Arrange the sprouts and the 'pigs in blankets' in a roasting tray (sheet pan). Place the tray in the hot oven and cook for 8–10 minutes or until the bacon is crispy. Remove the tray from the oven and set aside to cool. Slice each sausage in half lengthways.

Warm 2 tablespoons oil in a large frying pan (skillet) over a medium heat. Add the diced onion and carrots and cook for 5–6 minutes or until the onion is golden and the carrots have softened. Add the minced turkey and cook until browned, breaking it up with the back of wooden spoon in the pan.

Place the gravy granules in a measuring jug (pitcher) and add the boiling water. Stir until fully dissolved and a thick gravy is formed. Reduce the heat to low, pour the gravy into the frying pan and gently simmer for 2 minutes. Then add the cranberry sauce and stir until fully incorporated. Remove the pan from the heat and set aside.

Place the potatoes in a saucepan, cover with water and bring to the boil. Simmer gently for 5 minutes to parboil. Drain and set aside for later.

To make the bread sauce, stud the whole onion with the cloves and then place in a separate saucepan along with the bay leaf, peppercorns, ground nutmeg and milk. Place over a low heat and bring to the boil. Once boiling, remove from the heat and

For the bread sauce

1 onion, peeled

8 whole cloves

1 bay leaf

8 whole black peppercorns

½ teaspoon ground nutmeg

600ml (20¼fl oz) milk

125g (4½oz) white breadcrumbs

Salt and freshly ground black pepper

leave to rest for 15 minutes. Pass the infused milk through a sieve (strainer) and return it to the saucepan. Discard the onion and spices. Add the breadcrumbs to the milk and return to a low heat. Cook for 5 minutes or until all the liquid has been absorbed. Season with salt and pepper. Remove the pan from the heat and set aside.

Prepare the stuffing following the instructions on the packet, but leave it in a bowl rather than rolling it into balls.

Cover the base of a 30 x 23-cm (12 x 9-inch) deep-sided ovenproof dish with a layer of the potato slices. Top with half of the minced turkey, then scatter over half of the sliced sausages followed by the Brussels sprouts. Crumble over half of the chestnut stuffing. Cover everything with half of the bread sauce. Repeat these layers once more. Finish with a third layer of potato slices. Brush the remaining oil over the top of the potato.

Place the ovenproof dish on a baking tray and bake in the hot oven for 40 minutes or until the lasagne is golden and bubbling.

Remove the dish from the oven and scatter over the thyme or sage leaves, then allow the lasagne to rest for 10 minutes before slicing and serving with cranberry sauce and extra gravy.

COOK'S TIP This makes a lovely Boxing Day meal made from leftovers from Christmas dinner. Use cold turkey meat instead of the minced meat and add in any other vegetables you have left from your Christmas Day feast.

WIMBLEDON LASAGNE

With copious strawberries and Pimm's consumed each year, while aces are served and drop shots are fired, the Wimbledon Championship is an important fixture in British culinary and sporting calendars. This dish is in honour of the iconic tournament – and two-time men's singles champion, Andy Murray (one of my dream dinner-party guests).

Serves 4

For the shortbread

165g (5¾oz) butter, softened

80g (3oz) caster (superfine) sugar, plus extra for finishing

250g (9oz) plain (all-purpose) flour, plus extra for dusting

1 teaspoon vanilla extract

For the Pimm's cream

300ml (10½fl oz) double (heavy) cream

25g (¾oz) caster (superfine) sugar

50ml (1¾fl oz) Pimm's (or orange juice for an alcohol-free version)

To serve

300g (10½oz) strawberries, hulled and halved

Handful of fresh mint leaves, finely shredded, plus a sprig to decorate

1 tablespoon icing (confectioners') sugar

In a large mixing bowl, beat together the butter and caster sugar. Stir in the flour until well combined. Add the vanilla extract, then lightly knead the dough and gather it into one firm ball.

Lightly flour a piece of parchment paper. Place the dough on the parchment paper and roll it out into a rectangle measuring approx. 27 x 20 cm (10½ x 8 inches) and 1.5cm (½ inch) thick. Lightly score two lines across the dough, dividing it into three smaller 20 x 9-cm (8 x 3½-inch) rectangles (this makes it easier to cut to size once baked). Prick the dough all over with a fork. Lift the parchment paper and transfer the dough to a baking sheet. Chill in the fridge for 20 minutes.

Preheat the oven to 200°C/180°C fan/390°F/gas 6.

Bake in the oven for 12–15 minutes or until golden brown.

Remove from the oven. Immediately divide the shortbread into three smaller rectangles, cutting along the scored lines. Sprinkle with a little caster sugar and transfer to a wire rack to cool.

Pour the cream into a large mixing bowl, add the caster sugar and Pimm's and whisk to soft peaks.

To assemble immediately before serving, place one of the shortbread slabs on a serving dish or platter. Spread over half of the Pimm's cream and top with half of the strawberries and a few mint leaf shreds. Repeat these layers once more. Finish with the third shortbread slab. Dust the top with icing sugar and decorate with a sprig of mint leaves. Serve straight away so that the shortbread remains crisp.

ST DAVID'S RAREBIT LASAGNE

A perfect weekend brunch treat to be enjoyed on a lazy morning with friends. This recipe is an homage to the classic Welsh rarebit, but with inspiration taken from other international cuisines; the boozy cheese sauce is a staple of Wales while the croissant layer gives the dish a continental spin. This crispy, creamy, cheesy lasagne will likely become a firm favourite.

Serves 4

6 large croissants, halved lengthways

6–8 cooked ham slices (approx. 225g/8oz)

Small handful of chopped parsley, to serve (optional)

For the cheesy leek sauce

2 tablespoons vegetable oil

1 leek, halved lengthways and thinly sliced

75g (2½oz) salted butter

75g (2½oz) plain (all-purpose) flour

330ml (11fl oz) brown ale, at room temperature

1 tablespoon Worcestershire sauce

2 teaspoons Dijon mustard

260g (9½oz) mature Cheddar cheese, grated (shredded)

175ml (6fl oz) double (heavy) cream

Preheat the oven to 200°C/180°C fan/390°F/gas 6.

Heat the oil in a frying pan (skillet) over a medium heat. Add the sliced leeks and cook for 5 minutes or until softened. Remove the pan from the heat and set aside for later.

Melt the butter in a saucepan over a medium heat, then tip in the flour. Whisk continuously until the mixture comes away from the edges of the pan and then cook for a further 1 minute. Reduce the heat to low, gradually pour in the ale and whisk to form a thick sauce. Next, add the Worcestershire sauce and mustard, whisking all the time to ensure the sauce does not stick to the pan. Finally, add 225g (8oz) grated cheese and, whisking continuously, simmer on a low heat for a further 2 minutes.

Remove the pan from the heat and gradually stir in the cream to loosen the cheesy sauce slightly, then add the cooked leeks and stir to fully combine.

Cover the base of a 25 x 20-cm (10 x 8-inch) ovenproof dish with four of the croissant halves. Trim them to fit the dish, if necessary. Top with half of the leek sauce and half of the ham slices. Repeat the layers once more. Finish with a third layer of croissants. Scatter the remaining cheese over the top of the croissants.

Place the dish in the hot oven and cook for 15 minutes or until melted and golden. Cover the dish with foil and return to the oven for a further 10–15 minutes until bubbling.

Remove the dish from the oven and set aside for 5 minutes before scattering over the chopped parsley, if using, and serving.

CORONATION CHICKEN LASAGNE

While I was writing this book, coronation fever hit the UK with the crowning of King Charles III. Coronation chicken was invented in 1953 for the investiture of Queen Elizabeth II, so I have updated it for modern times. Bursting with the characteristic flavours that we all know and love, this one-dish take means that you can rustle up this dish in no more than 10 minutes.

Serves 3–4

200g (7oz) mayonnaise

75g (2½oz) crème fraîche

100g (3½oz) mango chutney

1 tablespoon mild
curry powder

1 teaspoon ground turmeric

50g (1¾oz) raisins

25g (¾oz) flaked (slivered)
almonds

3 cooked chicken breasts,
roughly chopped

½ iceberg lettuce,
roughly chopped

90g (3oz) pomegranate seeds

1½ tablespoons pomegranate
molasses

3 large tortilla wraps

Place the mayonnaise, crème fraîche, mango chutney, curry powder and turmeric in a large mixing bowl. Stir to combine fully. Next, add the raisins, almonds and chicken pieces and fold into the curry mayo.

In a separate bowl, combine the chopped lettuce and pomegranate seeds. Stir in 1 tablespoon pomegranate molasses to fully coat the salad.

Cover the base of a 23cm (9-inch) diameter dish with one tortilla wrap. Spoon half of the coronation chicken mixture over the wrap, then top with half the dressed salad.

Repeat these layers of tortilla warp, coronation chicken and salad once more. Finish with a third tortilla wrap and drizzle over the remaining pomegranate molasses.

COOK'S TIP The pomegranate molasses is a lovely touch, but it isn't essential. You can use a simple olive oil and balsamic dressing instead to dress the salad.

BURNS NIGHT LASAGNE

'So deep in love am I with this lasagne' is a line Robert Burns may have written had he tried this recipe. Created to honour the Scottish Bard's birthday, it features the elements of a traditional Burns Night supper: haggis, neeps and tatties, as it is fondly known in Scotland. There's a fine whisky sauce, too. Don't save this lasagne just for 25 January, you can serve it on Hogmanay too.

Serves 6–8

4 tablespoons vegetable oil

1 onion, finely diced

1 swede (rutabaga), peeled and diced into 1-cm (⅓-inch) cubes

2 carrots, peeled and diced into 1-cm (⅓-inch) cubes

3 celery sticks, diced into 1-cm (⅓-inch) cubes

2 teaspoons dried oregano

1 bay leaf

450g (1lb) haggis or vegetarian haggis, removed from the skin

2 x 400-g (14-oz) cans chopped tomatoes

1 leek, halved and finely sliced

125ml (4½fl oz) whisky

40g (1½oz) butter

40g (1½oz) plain (all-purpose) flour

330ml (11fl oz) milk

175ml (6fl oz) double (heavy) cream

900g (2lb) Maris Piper potatoes, peeled and cut into 3-mm (⅛-inch) thick slices

Preheat the oven to 200°C/180°C fan/390°F/gas 6.

Warm 2 tablespoons oil in a frying pan (skillet) over a medium heat. Add the onion and cook for 3 minutes or until softened. Next, add the swede, carrots and celery and leave to cook for 15 minutes, stirring occasionally. Reduce the heat to low and add the herbs.

Crumble the haggis into the pan and cook, stirring continuously, for 2 minutes. Pour in the chopped tomatoes, then rinse out the cans with 100ml (3½fl oz) cold water and add that too. Simmer for 10 minutes or until the vegetables are softened. Discard the bay leaf.

Place 2 tablespoons oil in a separate frying pan and warm over a medium heat. Add the leek and cook for 5 minutes. Reduce the heat to low and add 100ml (3½fl oz) whisky. Simmer for 2–3 minutes or until the whisky has reduced and leek has softened.

Combine the butter and flour in a saucepan over a low heat. Gradually pour in the milk, stirring continuously as the sauce thickens. Remove from the heat and stir in the cream. Return the pan to the heat briefly and add the leek and any excess liquid. Finally, stir in the remaining 25ml (¾fl oz) whisky. Set aside for later.

Cover the base of a 25 x 20-cm (10 x 8-inch) ovenproof dish with a layer of potato slices. Spoon over half of the haggis mixture followed by one-third of the leek sauce. Repeat these layers once more. Finish with a layer of potato slices and top with leek sauce.

Bake in the hot oven for 40 minutes. Cover the dish with foil, return to the oven and cook for a further 30 minutes or until the potatoes are soft. Set aside for 5 minutes before slicing and serving.

PUMPKIN, PECAN AND MAPLE TRAYBAKE

This traybake is a wonderful autumnal treat, when squashes are in season and the pumpkin harvest is in full swing. This recipe takes inspiration from the iconic pumpkin pie with its quirky combination of sweet and savoury flavours, in the style of a classic American dish. Enjoy this flaky and gooey traybake with a scoop or two of vanilla ice cream or a good glug of cream.

Serves 6–8

1 pumpkin or crown prince squash (approx. 1kg/2lb 3oz), halved and deseeded (or use 2 x 400-g/14-oz cans pumpkin purée)

1 teaspoon mixed spice

3 tablespoons maple syrup, plus extra for drizzling

130g (4½oz) pecans, roughly chopped

3 tablespoons butter, melted

1 x 270-g (9½-oz) packet filo (phyllo) pastry (approx. 5 sheets)

Vanilla ice cream or single (pure) cream, to serve

Preheat the oven to 200°C/180°C fan/390°F/gas 6.

Place the pumpkin halves on a baking sheet, cut side down, and roast in the preheated oven for 40 minutes or until the flesh is soft. Scoop out the flesh into a large bowl and set aside to cool.

Once cool, blend the pumpkin flesh to a smooth purée using a handheld stick (immersion) blender. Add the mixed spice and maple syrup, then stir through the pumpkin purée.

Brush the base of a 25 x 20-cm (10 x 8-inch) roasting tray (sheet pan) or ovenproof dish with a little melted butter. Lay three sheets of filo pastry over the base of the dish. Trim the sheets to fit the dish, if necessary. Brush each sheet with butter before adding the next one. (Keep the remaining sheets covered when not in use to prevent them drying out.) Spoon half of the pumpkin purée over the pastry. Set aside 20g (¾oz) of the chopped pecans, then scatter half of the remaining nuts over the pumpkin purée. Repeat these layers once more. Finish with a final layer of pastry, brushed with the remaining melted butter.

Bake in the hot oven for 30 minutes. Remove the dish from the oven and drizzle over some maple syrup and scatter over the remaining pecans. Return to the oven for a further 10 minutes until the filo is crispy and the nuts are toasted.

Let the traybake cool for a few minutes before slicing and serving warm with ice cream or cream.

COOK'S TIP The pumpkin season is short, but you can make this traybake using alternatives, such as a butternut squash.

ST PATRICK'S DAY CHOCOLATE AND STOUT LAYER CAKE

Recognised around the world as day for celebrating the shamrock, St Patrick's Day should be filled with leprechauns, limericks and, of course, pints of stout. With Irish dry stout in the cake mixture and Irish whiskey cream liqueur in the cream topping, this recipe couldn't be any more Irish. It's the perfect centrepiece for any St Paddy's Day soirée.

Serves 8–10

For the cake

150g (5½oz) salted butter

225g (8oz) light soft brown sugar

3 eggs, beaten

2 teaspoons vanilla extract

300ml (10½fl oz) Irish dry stout

270g (9½oz) self-raising flour, sifted

30g (1oz) unsweetened cocoa powder, sifted

1 teaspoon baking powder

200g (7oz) chocolate sandwich cookies, finely crushed (optional)

For the cream topping

600ml (20¼fl oz) double (heavy) cream

1 tablespoon caster (superfine) sugar

3 tablespoons Irish whiskey cream liqueur

Preheat the oven to 200°C/180°C fan/390°F/gas 6 and line four 20-cm (8-inch) cake tins with parchment paper.

In a large mixing bowl, beat together the butter and brown sugar until light and fluffy.

Using a gentle touch to keep the air in the cake batter for a light sponge, carefully fold in the beaten eggs, vanilla extract and stout until just combined.

Next, add the sifted flour, cocoa powder and baking powder to the bowl and gently fold into the mixture.

Lastly, fold the crushed cookie crumbs through the cake batter.

Pour one-quarter of the cake batter into each of the prepared tins, spreading it out evenly and levelling the surface.

Bake in the preheated oven for 10–12 minutes until the cakes are cooked through. Test the cakes are fully cooked by checking they are springy to the touch. Remove the tins from the oven and leave the cakes to cool in the tins for a few minutes before turning out onto a wire rack. Leave to cool completely before assembling.

To make the cream topping, whisk together the cream and sugar in a bowl and slowly pour in the Irish whiskey cream liqueur, continuing until soft peaks form. Be careful not to over-beat the cream otherwise it may go grainy.

Continued overleaf

To decorate

50g (1¾oz) dark (bittersweet) chocolate

To assemble, place the first cake layer on a serving plate and cover it with one-quarter of the whipped cream topping. Repeat these layers three more times, finishing with a final layer of the cream topping.

To make the shamrock decorations, melt the chocolate either in a heatproof bowl set over a saucepan of boiling water or carefully in a microwave. Transfer the melted chocolate to a piping (pastry) bag with a tiny hole. Pipe shamrock outlines onto parchment paper and allow to set.

To decorate, carefully peel the shamrocks from the paper and lay them carefully on the top of the cake. Alternatively, scatter a handful of cookie crumbs over the top of the cake. Slice, serve and enjoy as part of your St Patrick's day celebrations.

COOK'S TIP If you do not have the right number of cake tins, divide the batter and bake the cake layers in batches.

HOT CROSS BUN AND MASALA CHAI LASAGNE

With notes of cardamom and ginger, the chai custard provides a comforting warmth while the hot cross buns are bursting with fruity flavours. This heartening Easter-time lasagne can be enjoyed on a cold spring day, giving you that feeling of a loving embrace.

Serves 4–6

300ml (10½fl oz) double (heavy) cream, plus extra to serve

250ml (9fl oz) milk

2–4 chai teabags (depending on your preferred strength)

4 eggs

30g (1oz) caster (superfine) sugar

6 hot cross buns, sliced in half

20g (¾oz) salted butter, softened

50g (1¾oz) pecans, chopped

50g (1¾oz) sultanas (golden raisins)

Pour the cream and milk into a saucepan, add the teabags and gently simmer over a low heat for 5 minutes. Remove the pan from the heat and allow to cool a little before removing and discarding the teabags.

Whisk the eggs and sugar together in a bowl to combine. Next, pour the chai milk mixture onto the beaten eggs, whisking continuously to prevent any curdling or scrambling.

Meanwhile, spread the hot cross bun halves with the butter before assembling the lasagne.

Cover the base of a 20-cm (8-inch) ovenproof frying pan (skillet) or dish with four of the buttered hot cross bun halves. Scatter over half of the nuts and sultanas. Repeat these layer once more. Finish with a third layer of buns, making sure the 'tops' of the buns are facing upwards. Pour the chai custard over the buns to fill the dish and leave to soak for 10 minutes.

Preheat the oven to 180°C/160°C fan/350°F/gas 4.

Place the ovenproof dish on a baking tray and bake in the hot oven for 20 minutes or until the custard is just set. Remove from the oven and allow to cool before serving with a glug of cream.

COOK'S TIP You can easily change up the flavours in this recipe. Use your favourite type of hot cross bun, whether that's traditional, chocolate orange or salted caramel. Experiment with different nuts, too, such as walnuts or hazelnuts. You could even add some left-over chocolate Easter egg – if you have any, that is.

THE LOVE LASAGNE

This layered dessert is the perfect finale to a romantic meal. Prepare the dish in advance, then whip it out of the fridge before serving and dust it with a little sugar to give it that 'chef's kiss'. Mwah! The alluring addition of raspberry liqueur to the cream is bound to win over that special someone.

Serves 2

1 x 320-g (11-oz) packet ready-rolled all-butter puff pastry

Icing (confectioners') sugar, for dusting

150g (5½oz) raspberries

200g (7oz) strawberries, hulled and quartered

100g (3½oz) blueberries

Edible rose petals, to decorate (optional)

For the raspberry cream

250ml (9fl oz) double (heavy) cream

1 teaspoon caster (superfine) sugar

3 tablespoons raspberry liqueur (or orange juice for an alcohol-free version)

Preheat the oven to 210°C/190°C fan/410°F/gas 6½.

Line a baking sheet with a piece of parchment paper. Unroll the puff pastry sheet and cut it into four equal rectangles. Dust the pastry with icing sugar and transfer to the lined baking sheet. Lay a second piece of parchment paper on top and rest a second baking sheet on top.

Bake the pastry in the hot oven for 14 minutes. Lift off the top baking sheet and remove the top piece of parchment paper. Return to the oven for a further 4 minutes or until golden all over.

Remove from the oven and allow the pastry to cool completely.

Place the cream and caster sugar in a mixing bowl and whisk until nearly stiff. Take care not to over-beat the cream – you don't want it to go grainy. Gently fold the raspberry liqueur into the whipped cream. Pile the raspberry cream into a piping (pastry) bag fitted with a wide nozzle.

Place one of the slabs of puff pastry on a serving dish or platter. Pipe one-third of the raspberry cream over the puff pastry in little blobs, scattering over the berries as you pipe.

Repeat these layers of puff pastry, raspberry cream and mixed berries three more times. Chill in the fridge until ready to serve.

Immediately before serving, remove the lasagne from the fridge and dust the top with a little icing sugar. Scatter over the edible rose petals, if using, to add that special finishing touch.

COOK'S TIP Add a dash of rosewater to the whipped cream for an extra hint of romance.

TOFFEE APPLE DONUT LASAGNE FOR BONFIRE NIGHT

'Remember, remember the fifth of November' for this delightfully naughty dish! A small bite goes a long way as this tempting traybake really hits the sweet spot. Sugary donuts layered with warmly spiced toffee apples and topped with creamy ricotta leave many licking their lips!

Serves 6

25g (¾oz) butter

5 Granny Smith apples, peeled, cored and thinly sliced

25g (¾oz) light muscovado (light brown) sugar

2 teaspoons ground cinnamon

250g (9oz) ricotta cheese

60g (2oz) icing (confectioners') sugar

1 teaspoon vanilla extract

1 large egg, beaten

200ml (7fl oz) milk

9 plain ring donuts (depending on size), halved like a bagel

100g (3½oz) fudge chunks

Melt the butter in a large saucepan with a lid over a low heat. Add the sliced apples, muscovado sugar and cinnamon and stir well. Cover the pan with the lid and cook the apples, stirring occasionally, for 5–10 minutes or until the apples have softened.

In a bowl, combine the ricotta, icing sugar and vanilla extract. Add the beaten egg and gradually whisk in the milk, beating well.

Meanwhile, preheat the oven to 200°C/180°C fan/390°F/gas 6.

Cover the base of a 25 x 20-cm (10 x 8-inch) ovenproof dish with a layer of the donut halves. Spoon over half of the cooked apples, including any of the liquid left in the saucepan. Scatter over one-third of the fudge chunks and top with half of the ricotta mixture.

Repeat the layers once more. Finish with a third layer of donut halves. Scatter over the remaining fudge chunks and leave the lasagne to soak for 15 minutes.

Cover the dish with foil and cook the lasagne in the hot oven for 15 minutes. Remove the foil and return to the oven for a further 10 minutes or until the top is golden.

Remove the dish from the oven and allow the lasagne to cool for 10 minutes before slicing and serving.

COOK'S TIP If you feel like adding a crunchy texture to contrast the gooey fudge, scatter over some roughly chopped nuts, such as pecans.

INDEPENDENCE DAY LASAGNE

Patience is a virtue with this recipe, but I promise that it pays off. You'll create an eye-catching yet scrumptious dessert that takes inspiration from the classic American treat of peanut butter and jelly. The salty pretzels provide the perfect 'sheet' between the soft layers in this sweet lasagne.

Serves 8–10

For the pretzel base

140g (5oz) butter

100g (3½oz) golden syrup

225g (8oz) salted pretzels, crushed

For the peanut fudge

1 x 400-g (14-oz) can condensed milk

140g (5oz) peanut butter (smooth or crunchy)

2 teaspoons vanilla extract

50g (1¾oz) butter

80g (3oz) icing (confectioners') sugar, sifted

For the jelly

1 x 135-g (5-oz) block raspberry jelly (jello), cut into cubes

285ml (9½fl oz) boiling water

To decorate

400ml (14fl oz) double (heavy) cream

90g (3oz) Reese's mini peanut butter cups, to decorate

Small handful of pretzels, kept whole

Line an 18-cm (7-inch) square cake tin with parchment paper or use a glass serving dish.

To prepare the pretzel base, melt 70g (2½oz) butter in a saucepan over a low heat, then stir in 50g (1¾oz) golden syrup. Tip in half the crushed pretzels and stir thoroughly to mix everything together. Pour the pretzel mixture into the prepared tin or dish and press down to form the base. Set aside.

Next, make the peanut fudge. In a saucepan over a low heat, place the condensed milk, peanut butter, vanilla extract and butter. Stir occasionally until the butter has melted and the fudge looks smooth and silky. Turn up the heat to medium and boil the fudge for 2 minutes, stirring continuously to prevent the mixture sticking. Remove the pan from the heat and add the icing sugar, stirring vigorously to combine. Pour the fudge into the tin or dish over the pretzel base and place in the fridge for at least 4 hours.

Make another pretzel layer in the same way with the remaining butter, golden syrup and crushed pretzels. Gently pour the pretzel mixture over the set peanut fudge layer and level it out.

Lastly, prepare the jelly. Place the jelly cubes in a measuring bowl or jug (pitcher). Add the boiling water and stir until dissolved. Add cold water to make it up to 570ml (19fl oz), stirring continuously until the jelly has dissolved. Pour the jelly over the pretzel layer and set in the fridge for at least 24 hours.

When you're ready to serve, whip the cream to soft peaks and spoon over the top jelly layer. Decorate the top with the mini Reese's cups and whole pretzels.

INDEX

A

amaretti and nectarine lasagne 90

apples: toffee apple donut lasagne for Bonfire Night 134

apricot, pistachio and chocolate ganache traybake 98

asparagus: pesto salmon and asparagus lasagne 54

aubergines (eggplants): mixed bean and ratatouille lasagne 71–2

    sausage, aubergine and Puy lentil lasagne 29

    spiced lamb lasagne 26

    tofu and sweet potato Massaman lasagne 82

B

bacon: full English breakfast lasagne 18

    loaded dirty burger lasagne 40–1

    ravioli lasagne 38

    venison, mushroom and fig lasagne 23

baked beans: chorizo, tomato, olive and gnocchi traybake 22

    full English breakfast lasagne 18

bakes: curried cod and cauliflower bake 50

    pulled pork nacho bake 17

banana and speculoos lasagne 104

beans: mixed bean and ratatouille lasagne 71–2

    see also baked beans

beef: loaded dirty burger lasagne 40–1

    roast dinner lasagne 30–3

spicy meatball lasagne 28

beetroot (beets), butternut and pecan lasagne 64–5

biscuits: chocolate s'mores bites 108

    shortbread 116

black bean, courgette and quinoa lasagne 81

black pudding: full English breakfast lasagne 18

blueberries: blueberry 'bread and butter' pudding with lemon curd 96

    the love lasagne 132

bread: banana and speculoos lasagne 104

bread sauce 112–13

'bread and butter' pudding, blueberry 96

broccoli: pesto salmon and asparagus lasagne 54

    salmon and pak choi lasagne 48

Brussels sprouts: Christmas dinner lasagne 112–13

burgers: loaded dirty burger lasagne 40–1

Burns Night lasagne 123

butternut squash: beetroot, butternut and pecan lasagne 64–5

C

cabbage: braised red cabbage 30–3

    falafel, halloumi and red cabbage stack 86

    pulled jackfruit, sweet potato and red cabbage lasagne 84

cakes: cherry and hazelnut meringue layer cake 100–2

    St Patrick's Day chocolate and stout layer cake 126–8

cannellini (white kidney) beans:

polenta, pepper and peanut lasagne 68–70

caramel: salted caramel and rice pudding lasagne 99

cashew butter: salmon and pak choi lasagne 48

cauliflower: cauliflower cheese 30–3

    curried cod and cauliflower bake 50

    roast dinner lasagne 30–3

chai tea: hot cross bun and masala chai lasagne 130

cheese: beetroot, butternut and pecan lasagne 64–5

    cauliflower cheese 30–3

    chicken quesadilla lasagne 34

    falafel, halloumi and red cabbage stack 86

    four mushroom and five cheese lasagne 76–8

    lamb, feta and filo lasagne 36–7

    loaded dirty burger lasagne 40–1

    macaroni cheese 40–1

    polenta, pepper and peanut lasagne 68–70

    pulled pork nacho bake 17

    roast dinner lasagne 30–3

    St David's rarebit lasagne 120

    sausage, aubergine and Puy lentil lasagne 29

    spicy meatball lasagne 28

    see also ricotta

cheesecake: cookies and cream lasagne 105

cherry and hazelnut meringue layer cake 100–2

chestnut stuffing: Christmas dinner lasagne 112–13

chicken: chicken, prune and pistachio lasagne 14

    chicken quesadilla lasagne 34

    chicken tikka 'masalasagne' 24

Coronation chicken lasagne 122

prawn, chicken and chorizo traybake 44

chips: fish and chips lasagne 46–7

chocolate: apricot, pistachio and chocolate ganache traybake 98

cherry and hazelnut meringue layer cake 100–2

chocolate s'mores bites 108

cookies and cream lasagne 105

espresso martini trifle 92

Independence Day lasagne 136

Neapolitan pots 95

St Patrick's Day chocolate and stout layer cake 126–8

chocolate sandwich cookies: St Patrick's Day chocolate and stout layer cake 126–8

chorizo: chorizo, tomato, olive and gnocchi traybake 22

prawn, chicken and chorizo traybake 44

Christmas dinner lasagne 112–13

coconut milk: halibut, mango and coconut lasagne 58

coffee: espresso martini trifle 92

cookies and cream lasagne 105

Coronation chicken lasagne 122

courgettes (zucchini): black bean, courgette and quinoa lasagne 81

mixed bean and ratatouille lasagne 71–2

ravioli lasagne 38

teriyaki salmon lasagne with courgette and quinoa 56

couscous: cod and Parma ham lasagne 52

cranberries: mincemeat, cranberry and orange traybake 109

cream: apricot, pistachio and chocolate ganache traybake 98

cookies and cream lasagne 105

hot cross bun and masala chai lasagne 130

Independence Day lasagne 136

Key lime shortbread stack 106

the love lasagne 132

Neapolitan pots 95

St Patrick's Day chocolate and stout layer cake 126–8

Wimbledon lasagne 116

cream cheese: cookies and cream lasagne 105

four mushroom and five cheese lasagne 76–8

Neapolitan pots 95

crêpes, rhubarb, elderflower and custard 94

crispy duck pancake lasagne 20

croissants: St David's rarebit lasagne 120

curry: chicken tikka 'masalasagne' 24

Coronation chicken lasagne 122

curried cod and cauliflower bake 50

halibut, mango and coconut lasagne 58

custard: blueberry 'bread and butter' pudding with lemon curd 96

espresso martini trifle 92

rhubarb, elderflower and custard crêpes 94

D

dahl: red lentil, spinach and dahl lasagne 74

digestive biscuits (graham crackers): chocolate s'mores bites 108

donuts, Bonfire Night toffee apple 134

duck: crispy duck pancake lasagne 20

E

eggs: full English breakfast lasagne 18

elderflower cordial: rhubarb, elderflower and custard crêpes 94

espresso martini trifle 92

F

falafel, halloumi and red cabbage stack 86

feta: lamb, feta and filo lasagne 36–7

figs: venison, mushroom and fig lasagne 23

filo (phyllo) pastry: lamb, feta and filo lasagne 36–7

pumpkin, pecan and maple traybake 124

fish 42–61

cod and Parma ham lasagne 52

curried cod and cauliflower bake 50

fish and chips lasagne 46–7

halibut, mango and coconut lasagne 58

harissa tuna lasagne 60

pesto salmon and asparagus lasagne 54

salmon and pak choi lasagne 48

teriyaki salmon lasagne with courgette and quinoa 56

fries: loaded dirty burger lasagne 40–1

full English breakfast lasagne 18

G

gnocchi: chorizo, tomato, olive and gnocchi traybake 22

H

haggis: Burns Night lasagne 123

halloumi: falafel, halloumi and red cabbage stack 86

ham: St David's rarebit lasagne 120

harissa tuna lasagne 60

hash browns: full English breakfast lasagne 18

hazelnuts: cherry and hazelnut meringue layer cake 100–2

hot cross bun and masala chai lasagne 130

hummus: falafel, halloumi and red cabbage stack 86

I

Independence Day lasagne 136

J

jackfruit: pulled jackfruit, sweet potato and red cabbage lasagne 84

K

Key lime shortbread stack 106

L

lamb: lamb, feta and filo lasagne 36–7

spiced lamb lasagne 26

lasagne: amaretti and nectarine lasagne 90

banana and speculoos lasagne 104

beetroot, butternut and pecan lasagne 64–5

black bean, courgette and quinoa lasagne 81

Burns Night lasagne 123

chicken, prune and pistachio lasagne 14

chicken quesadilla lasagne 34

Christmas dinner lasagne 112–13

cod and Parma ham lasagne 52

cookies and cream lasagne 105

Coronation chicken lasagne 122

crispy duck pancake lasagne 20

fish and chips lasagne 46–7

four mushroom and five cheese lasagne 76–8

full English breakfast lasagne 18

halibut, mango and coconut lasagne 58

harissa tuna lasagne 60

hot cross bun and masala chai lasagne 130

Independence Day lasagne 136

lamb, feta and filo lasagne 36–7

loaded dirty burger lasagne 40–1

the love lasagne 132

mixed bean and ratatouille lasagne 71–2

pesto salmon and asparagus lasagne 54

polenta, pepper and peanut lasagne 68–70

pulled jackfruit, sweet potato and red cabbage lasagne 84

ravioli lasagne 38

red lentil, spinach and dahl lasagne 74

roast dinner lasagne 30–3

St David's rarebit lasagne 120

salmon and pak choi lasagne 48

salted caramel and rice pudding lasagne 99

satay prawn noodle lasagne 49

sausage, aubergine and Puy lentil lasagne 29

spiced lamb lasagne 26

spicy meatball lasagne 28

sweet and sour pork lasagne 16

tofu and sweet potato Massaman lasagne 82

tofu, Puy lentil and spinach lasagne 80

venison, mushroom and fig lasagne 23

Wimbledon lasagne 116

lemon curd, blueberry 'bread and butter' pudding with 96

lentils: harissa tuna lasagne 60

red lentil, spinach and dahl lasagne 74

sausage, aubergine and Puy lentil lasagne 29

tofu, Puy lentil and spinach lasagne 80

limes: Key lime shortbread stack 106

loaded dirty burger lasagne 40–1

the love lasagne 132

M

macaroni cheese: loaded dirty burger lasagne 40–1

mango: halibut, mango and coconut lasagne 58

Neapolitan pots 95

marshmallows: chocolate s'mores bites 108

martini: espresso martini trifle 92

'masalasagne' 24

mascarpone cheese: banana and speculoos lasagne 104

cherry and hazelnut meringue layer cake 100–2

chocolate s'mores bites 108

cod and Parma ham lasagne 52

espresso martini trifle 92

Massaman lasagne, tofu and sweet potato 82

meatballs: spicy meatball lasagne 28

meringue layer cake, cherry and hazelnut 100–2

mincemeat, cranberry and orange traybake 109

muffins: blueberry 'bread and butter' pudding with lemon curd 96

espresso martini trifle 92

mushrooms: four mushroom and five cheese lasagne 76–8

full English breakfast lasagne 18

venison, mushroom and fig lasagne 23

N

naan breads: red lentil, spinach and dahl lasagne 74

nachos: pulled pork nacho bake 17

Neapolitan pots 95

nectarines: amaretti and nectarine lasagne 90

noodles: satay prawn noodle lasagne 49

O

olives: chorizo, tomato, olive and gnocchi traybake 22

oranges: mincemeat, cranberry and orange traybake 109

orzo: spiced lamb lasagne 26

P

pak choi: salmon and pak choi lasagne 48

pancakes: crispy duck pancake lasagne 20

pancetta: chicken, prune and pistachio lasagne 14

Parma ham: cod and Parma ham lasagne 52

pasta: beetroot, butternut and pecan lasagne 64–5

chicken, prune and pistachio lasagne 14

four mushroom and five cheese lasagne 76–8

halibut, mango and coconut lasagne 58

harissa tuna lasagne 60

loaded dirty burger lasagne 40–1

pesto salmon and asparagus lasagne 54

ravioli lasagne 38

spiced lamb lasagne 26

spicy meatball lasagne 28

tofu, Puy lentil and spinach lasagne 80

peanut butter: Independence Day lasagne 136

polenta, pepper and peanut lasagne 68–70

satay prawn noodle lasagne 49

peas: fish and chips lasagne 46–7

pecans: beetroot, butternut and pecan lasagne 64–5

pumpkin, pecan and maple traybake 124

peppers (bell): chicken quesadilla lasagne 34

chicken tikka 'masalasagne' 24

mixed bean and ratatouille lasagne 71–2

polenta, pepper and peanut lasagne 68–70

prawn, chicken and chorizo traybake 44

pulled pork nacho bake 17

ravioli lasagne 38

sweet and sour pork lasagne 16

pesto salmon and asparagus lasagne 54

Pimm's: Wimbledon lasagne 116

pineapple: Neapolitan pots 95

sweet and sour pork lasagne 16

pistachios: apricot, pistachio and chocolate ganache traybake 98

chicken, prune and pistachio lasagne 14

pita breads: falafel, halloumi and red cabbage stack 86

polenta, pepper and peanut lasagne 68–70

poppadoms: chicken tikka 'masalasagne' 24

pork: pulled pork nacho bake 17

sweet and sour pork lasagne 16

see also sausages

potatoes: Burns Night lasagne 123

Christmas dinner lasagne 112–13

curried cod and cauliflower bake 50

potato rösti 46–7

roast dinner lasagne 30–3

roast potatoes 30–3

venison, mushroom and fig lasagne 23

prawns (shrimps): prawn, chicken and chorizo traybake 44

satay prawn noodle lasagne 49

pretzels: Independence Day lasagne 136

prunes: chicken, prune and pistachio lasagne 14

puff pastry: the love lasagne 132

pulled jackfruit, sweet potato and red cabbage lasagne 84

pulled pork nacho bake 17

pumpkin, pecan and maple traybake 124

Q

quesadilla lasagne, chicken 34

quinoa: black bean, courgette and quinoa lasagne 81

teriyaki salmon lasagne with courgette and quinoa 56

R

rarebit lasagne, St David's 120

raspberries: cookies and cream lasagne 105

the love lasagne 132

raspberry jelly (jello): Independence Day lasagne 136

ratatouille: mixed bean and ratatouille lasagne 71–2

ravioli lasagne 38

refried beans: chicken quesadilla lasagne 34

rhubarb, elderflower and custard crêpes 94

rice: prawn, chicken and chorizo traybake 44

sweet and sour pork lasagne 16

rice pudding: salted caramel and rice pudding lasagne 99

ricotta: toffee apple donut lasagne for Bonfire Night 134

fish and chips lasagne 46–7

loaded dirty burger lasagne 40–1

spiced lamb lasagne 26

spicy meatball lasagne 28

roast dinner lasagne 30–3

roti: chicken tikka 'masalasagne' 24

S

St David's rarebit lasagne 120

St Patrick's Day chocolate and stout layer cake 126–8

salted caramel and rice pudding lasagne 99

satay prawn noodle lasagne 49

sausages: Christmas dinner lasagne 112–13

full English breakfast lasagne 18

sausage, aubergine and Puy lentil lasagne 29

shortbread: Key lime shortbread stack 106

Wimbledon lasagne 116

s'mores, chocolate 108

speculoos spread: banana and speculoos lasagne 104

spiced lamb lasagne 26

spicy meatball lasagne 28

spinach: red lentil, spinach and dahl lasagne 74

tofu, Puy lentil and spinach lasagne 80

squash: beetroot, butternut and pecan lasagne 64–5

stack, falafel, halloumi and red cabbage 86

strawberries: the love lasagne 132

Wimbledon lasagne 116

strawberry jam (preserve): Neapolitan pots 95

stout: St Patrick's Day chocolate and stout layer cake 126–8

sultanas (golden raisins): hot cross bun and masala chai lasagne 130

swede: Burns Night lasagne 123

sweet and sour pork lasagne 16

sweet potatoes: pulled jackfruit, sweet potato and red cabbage lasagne 84

tofu and sweet potato Massaman lasagne 82

T

Tenderstem broccoli: pesto salmon and asparagus lasagne 54

teriyaki salmon lasagne with courgette and quinoa 56

tikka 'masalasagne', chicken 24

toffee apple donut lasagne for Bonfire Night 134

tofu: tofu and sweet potato Massaman lasagne 82

tofu, Puy lentil and spinach lasagne 80

tomatoes: chorizo, tomato, olive and gnocchi traybake 22

full English breakfast lasagne 18

tortilla chips: pulled pork nacho bake 17

tortilla wraps: chicken quesadilla lasagne 34

Coronation chicken lasagne 122

traybakes: apricot, pistachio and chocolate ganache traybake 98

chorizo, tomato, olive and gnocchi traybake 22

mincemeat, cranberry and orange traybake 109

prawn, chicken and chorizo traybake 44

pumpkin, pecan and maple traybake 124

trifle, espresso martini 92

turkey: Christmas dinner lasagne 112–13

V

vegetables: roast dinner lasagne 30–3

venison, mushroom and fig lasagne 23

W

whisky: Burns Night lasagne 123

Wimbledon lasagne 116

Y

Yorkshire pudding wraps: roast dinner lasagne 30–3

ACKNOWLEDGEMENTS

Around 99.9% of my family and friends had no idea I was writing this book. Many believed the 'lasagne chapter' of my life quietly ended with the TV show. So, I'd like to start by apologising to all those whose questions I evaded for some time. I hope this makes up for the secrecy.

To start where it all began, I have to thank the flatmates and university friends present at the now infamous Christmas dinner. Then to the friend who suggested I apply for *The Great Cookbook Challenge* and was a champion of the Christmas Dinner lasagne, having been present at its inauguration.

To Jamie Oliver, Channel 4 and Plum Productions (especially the producers and camera crew) who made my time on the show so special. There I was able to hone my book idea which led me to my agent, Heather Holden-Brown, who I've got to thank for guiding me throughout this process. And then to my publisher, Céline Hughes, and the whole team at Murdoch Books, thank you for believing in my novel idea and for bringing my recipes to page and print. I am indebted to the editor, Lisa, food stylist, Becci, photographer, Steve, and designer, Dave, who have all crafted this stunning masterpiece.

To everyone I surreptitiously tested recipes on throughout the first six months of 2023, whether that be hosting suppers, doorstop drop-offs or my insistence on bringing a dish to parties. I am so grateful that no-one ever questioned why everything I produced was in some form of layers!

To the few friends, both in the UK and abroad, I confided in and who supported me through the late nights of recipe writing or early morning supermarket shops. I'll never forget the sacrifice you each made in keeping this secret while providing me with laughter and copious cups of tea to get me through the challenging times of juggling working as a doctor and writing a book.

Finally, I'd like to thank those who have shaped me into the cook I am today, from aunts and a beloved grannie through to the phenomenal wedding team I was part of for over a decade. But most importantly, my mum who taught me all I know about the fundamentals of food, who allowed me to bake a cake over and over until I'd perfected it and willingly got up at 5am to supervise me rustling up a batch of scones before driving me to a far-flung baking competition. And not forgetting my Dad's contribution to my culinary knowledge: SPAM, baked beans and chips!

RECIPE NOTES

Eggs are always medium (UK)/large (Aus/US).

Butter is always unsalted, unless specified otherwise.

Herbs are always fresh, unless specified otherwise.

Both metric and imperial measures are used in this book. Follow one set of measurements throughout, not a mixture, as they are not interchangeable.

All spoon measurements are level, unless specified otherwise.

Tablespoon measures: We have used 15ml (3 teaspoon) tablespoon measures.

Oven guide: You may find cooking times vary depending on your oven. The recipes in this book are based on fan-assisted oven temperatures. For non-fan-assisted ovens, as a general rule, set the oven temperature to 20°C (35°F) higher than indicated in the recipe.

Published in 2024 by Murdoch Books, an imprint of Allen & Unwin

Murdoch Books UK
Ormond House
26–27 Boswell Street
London WC1N 3JZ
Phone: +44 (0) 20 8785 5995
murdochbooks.co.uk
info@murdochbooks.co.uk

Murdoch Books Australia
Cammeraygal Country
83 Alexander Street
Crows Nest NSW 2065
Phone: +61 (0)2 8425 0100
murdochbooks.com.au
info@murdochbooks.com.au

For corporate orders and custom publishing, contact our business development team at salesenquiries@murdochbooks.com.au

Publisher: Céline Hughes
Project Editor: Lisa Pendreigh
Designer: Dave Brown
Photographer and Props Stylist: Steve Painter
Food Stylist: Rebecca Woods
Production Director, UK: Niccolò De Bianchi
Production Director, Australia: Lou Playfair

Text © Sarah Wordie 2024
The moral right of the author has been asserted.
Design © Murdoch Books 2024
Photography © Steve Painter 2024

Murdoch Books Australia acknowledges the Traditional Owners of the Country on which we live and work. We pay our respects to all Aboriginal and Torres Strait Islander Elders, past and present.

ISBN 9781922616937

 A catalogue record for this book is available from the National Library of Australia

A catalogue record for this book is available from the British Library

Colour reproduction by Born Group, London, UK
Printed by 1010 Printing International Limited, China

10 9 8 7 6 5 4 3 2 1

MIX
Paper | Supporting responsible forestry
FSC® C016973